INTRODUCTION TO PRIVATE INVESTIGATIONS

Private Investigator Entry Level (02E)

ISBN: 0615847714
ISBN-13: 978-0615847719

For Melissa, Philip, and Ava

CONTENTS

Introduction to Conducting Private Investigations
Private Investigator Entry Level (02E)

Acknowledgements

A heartfelt thank you to everyone who made this book possible, including those sounding-boards and editors who graciously sacrificed their time for my benefit. In particular, I'd like to thank Andrew Schroeder, Scott Krischke, my wife Melissa, and my father Philip Becnel III. Thank you to David Williams, for his spectacular work on the illustrations in this book. Lastly, thank you to my business partners at Dinolt Becnel & Wells Investigative Group LLC, Benjamin Dinolt, Brendan Wells, and Pierre Russell, and to the many other people who contributed to this project in ways large and small. I could not have written this book without your generous support and guidance.

Introduction

I wrote the first edition of this textbook as an entry-level resource for Private Investigator Entry Level (02E), the course mandated for all private investigator registrants in the Commonwealth of Virginia. After the first edition was published I received feedback from private investigators all over the country telling me that my book was an unmatched resource for their practices, too, and not only for Virginia investigators. Therefore, when I was asked to publish a second edition I considered how I could make the book even more applicable to investigators throughout the United States, while still maintaining its use as a textbook for the 02E course.

The most obvious addition was to include a synopsis of each state's private investigation licensing laws in Part I (Orientation). Whereas the first edition focused primarily on Virginia licensing laws, this book separates all state licensing laws into several categories, from states that do not require licensing to those that require a background check, a minimum amount of experience, training, or a combination thereof. While there are a few online resources for this information (some of which I used to research my additions to this textbook), I am unaware of any book that summarizes each state's laws in the manner that I have. What I have accomplished, I believe, is as close to a comprehensive summary of all the state private investigation licensing laws as exists anywhere in print.

It goes without saying that some laws and technology have inevitably changed since the first edition was published. For example, there was a major U.S. Supreme Court decision on global positioning system (GPS) trackers, and this was a game-changer for how private investigators throughout the country use GPS trackers. One of the reasons I took the opportunity to write the second edition of this textbook was that I could not live with the idea that something I wrote was no longer true. I combed through the first edition in painstaking detail to correct areas where law and technology have changed the playing field during the past two years. Likewise, many of the web links I included in the first edition are no longer active. I chose to remove many of these links, rather than update them, because I realized the same problem would inevitably happen again before I have the opportunity to publish a third edition.

I have also learned a lot since the first edition was published. My practice is constantly growing and evolving. For example, I published a book in 2012, titled *Principles of Investigative Documentation*,[1] and writing that book made me rethink some of the documentation practices I included in the first edition of *Introduction to Conducting Private Investigations*. Over time I developed better ways of performing certain investigative tasks, and I wanted the second edition to reflect what I have learned. Many of these changes are subtle and may not be noticeable by those who read the first edition. Others represent major changes in how I have come to see the value in certain types of information. The most widespread changes are in Part II (Investigative Skills) and Part III (Documentation), where I increased the emphasis on evidence available through social media.

What remains from the first edition is as relevant now as it was the day I first wrote it, and I left those portions unchanged. The genesis for the book is still implicit in its pages. My goal was to write a textbook that would be a valuable resource for entry-level investigators. Before I wrote the first edition, I had been teaching criminal justice courses as an adjunct instructor at a local college for over a year and became certified to teach the 02E course in Virginia. As an adjunct instructor, I taught courses on criminal procedure, criminal investigation, and white collar crime. In teaching these courses, I drew on my Master's degree in criminal justice and over a decade of experience working as a private investigator in the Washington, D.C. area. I also relied on the excellent lesson plans and textbooks provided by the university. When I began teaching the 02E course, I was surprised to learn there were no textbooks related exclusively to conducting private investigations. While there were a few specialty books on different aspects of the field, there were no entry-level textbooks that covered all the areas required by the Department of Criminal Justice Services (DCJS), the agency that regulates private investigators in Virginia.[2] The first edition of this book was an attempt to provide such a textbook for students and instructors of the sixty-two or so (at the time) private security schools certified to teach the 02E in Virginia.

In this book I have attempted to balance the theoretical with the practical. I learned as an instructor that theory often spurs classroom discussion concerning the salient legal and ethical issues of our profession. But theory is often the missing component in private security classrooms since 02E courses are often taught by practitioners with extensive experience, but little conceptual education in private investigations. I wrote this book to help practitioner-instructors incorporate concepts and theories with their own real-world experiences. Accordingly, instructors should maintain their own lesson plans and supplement them with readings from this book. By assigning readings and exercises that complement their own learning objectives, students will benefit more from the lessons.

I also wrote this book to be readable and entertaining. Many of the case studies and descriptions of different types of investigations are drawn from my firm's cases. Like most private investigators, I have developed certain niches and areas of expertise during my career.[3] Most of my billable time during the past five years has been spent conducting investigations and behavioral analysis interviews in employment litigation matters. My goal in writing these narratives was never to brag about my experiences or to claim that I know everything there is to know about each type of investigation. Rather, I have provided case studies and examples for the enjoyment and education of the student, and for instructors to supplement their own experiences as necessary.

As I discuss in the text, Virginia regulations make it illegal to disclose facts about a particular case to third parties without the client's written permission.[4] Because some of the cases discussed in this book occurred many years ago, it was impractical to contact each client to obtain written permission. Therefore, I remained in compliance with the law by largely fictionalizing the facts in each case, thereby making them unrecognizable to any parties involved. Some of the examples represent the facts of several cases merged together, and other examples are completely fictional. In other words, although the scenarios herein do represent actual cases worked by myself or my firm's investigators, they are not verbatim examples. I did this not to embellish my experience or to make the cases more interesting to the reader—but solely to protect the confidentiality of the clients and other parties involved.

This book is organized around the main topics mandated by the Department of Criminal Justice Services, and then separated into individual chapters as required by necessity. Although I introduce and order the topics in a way that should be logical and clear to entry-level private investigations students, the topics are distinct enough that instructors can assign readings from the book in any order they see fit. This text-book is organized into five parts, which mirror the subjects required for registration in Virginia. Although the book was structured to make it easy for use in DCJS-compliant courses, the content is equally applicable to private investigators anywhere in the United States.

Part I (Orientation) begins by clearly defining the role of the private investigator. It differentiates the private investigator from other types of investigators in American society, and discusses the legal require-ments that define and govern the profession. There is also a summary of each state's private investigation licensing laws, including the laws of Washington, D.C. Part I also explores the ethical dilemmas that arise from the nature of the profession and discusses the ethical standards that resolve these predicaments. The private investigative field is fraught with moral pitfalls that require an investigator to exercise self-consciousness with regard to her professional role in society. It is an axiom that a private investigator's ethics will be challenged in the course of practicing her profession, and successfully traversing these challenges requires an unyielding moral compass, as well as a solid grounding on issues of misrepresentation, bias, conflicts of interest, and confidentiality.

Part II (Investigative Skills) begins by detailing the methodical system of problem solving at the core of the profession, and then introduces the technical skills necessary to conduct investigations: research, inter-viewing, and surveillance. By having a disciplined and systematic ap-proach to her investigations, and having an investigative toolbox stocked with all the knowledge and experience required to employ each of the divergent methods of gathering evidence, an investigator should be well-equipped to solve any problem.

Part III (Documentation) discusses the methods of managing and documenting investigations for clients. On a fundamental level, private investigation is the business of selling investigative reports to custom-ers. Clients unsatisfied with the quality of an investigator's reports will seek investigative services elsewhere. The ability to solve problems is not sufficient; evidence must be properly documented to be actionable in court and to justify the costs associated with conducting private in-vestigations. An investigator must have thorough knowledge of how to collect and document real evidence, and how and when to take sworn statements and declarations from witnesses.

Part IV (Types of Investigations) details the different types of investi-gations that a private investigator may be hired to conduct. The book specifically addresses the eight different types of investigations named in the DCJS requirements: background, missing persons, criminal, undercover, fraud and financial, insurance, domestic, and accident investigations. However, we could have defined the types of investigations differently. For example, we could have instead discussed investigations concerning various types of litigation or internal investigations, and in many ways this may have been more applicable to the types of investigations that private investigators routinely perform. Although the universe of "types" of investigations is practically boundless, an investigator should be prepared to conduct any investigation, anywhere: ethically, legally, logically, and competently.

Part V (The Law of Investigations) addresses the legal restrictions pertaining to how a private investigator may conduct investigations, including laws relating to privacy. Additionally, Part V discusses a number of constitutional rules—those governing search and seizure, and the privilege against self-incrimination, for example—that formally apply only to law enforcement (i.e., "public") investigators, but that any private investigator must also understand as background in her own investigations. Additionally, Part V provides background on the structure and inner-workings of both the state and federal court systems, the rules regarding service of process, and the myriad types of civil parties and corporate structures. As a gatherer of evidence, an investigator must understand the rules regarding the admissibility of evidence into court proceedings.

While writing the book, I kept the learning objectives for the 02E course at the forefront. DCJS requires instructors to incorporate learning objectives in each course, and it is these learning objectives that become the basis of the exam that all students must pass with a score of at least seventy percent in order to become registered private investigators.[5] While instructors may want to employ their own learning objectives in their classrooms, this book is intended to teach students the following:

- The general knowledge required to conduct background investigations
- The ethical standards required of private investigators
- The basic private investigation licensing requirements for different jurisdictions in the United States

- The definition of a private investigator as specified by the Virginia Code, and what distinguishes being a private investigator as a professional identity
- The importance of avoiding misrepresentation and bias during investigations; identifying and avoiding conflicts of interest; upholding confidentiality; and maintaining sound business practices
- The general methods of conducting missing persons investigations
- The relevant principles and theories of the U.S. Constitution and the rule of law, including the landmark concept of what entails a reasonable expectation of privacy, and other legal safeguards proscribed by the Fourth and Fifth Amendments
- The general knowledge required to conduct criminal investigations
- The respective jurisdictions of state and federal court systems; the rules and legal theories regarding service of process; the various types of civil parties and corporate structures; and the procedures for criminal and civil actions, from filing to appeal
- The rules of evidence
- The major state and federal laws related to privacy and employment protection
- The general information required to conduct undercover investigations
- How to conduct investigations using the scientific method
- How to conduct investigative research, including court records retrieval and online database searches
- The general information required to conduct fraud and financial investigations
- How to conduct interviews and interpret behavioral symptoms of deception
- The general information required to conduct insurance investigations
- How to conduct covert and overt surveillance
- The general information required to conduct domestic investigations
- The methods, and importance, of documentation during investigations, including note taking, report writing, and testimony
- The methods of gathering real evidence
- How to take sworn statements and declarations from witnesses
- The general information required to conduct accident investigations

This textbook admittedly does not explain everything there is to know about conducting private investigations, but it provides a framework for learning the field through the O2E or similar private investigations course. As with any trade or profession, students will grow into investigators with practice from real investigations. Students learn best by doing—not listening or reading. When I teach class, I always incorporate as many practical exercises as possible to help simulate this real world experience. For example, when I teach constitutional law to undergraduate students, I conduct an exercise where they are required to complete an affidavit in support of a search warrant to establish probable cause, and then conduct a search of my car in the parking lot. Inside my car, students find various "contraband," which they must catalog in an inventory. Such an exercise encapsulates the implications of the Fourth Amendment more effectively than reading a textbook or listening to a lecture. The exercises and questions dispersed throughout this textbook are ones that I have found most helpful in driving home the learning objectives in my courses.

The end result, I hope, is an interesting and informative textbook drawn heavily from my experience as an investigator and instructor, with a good balance between theory and practice. While the book is intended first and foremost as an instructional tool, it also represents a personal apex, an implicit memoir outlining much of my investigative experience to date. It was my (perhaps grandiose) hope that by chronicling my experiences in this textbook, I could raise the bar on the instructional quality of private investigation courses across the country, and thereby set higher standards for private investigators everywhere.

Philip A. Becnel IV

Part I
Orientation

1

The Private Investigation Profession

Private Investigator: Any individual who engages in the business of, or accepts employment to make, investigations to obtain information on crimes or civil wrongs; the location, disposition, or recovery of stolen property; the cause of accidents, fires, damages, or injuries to persons or to property; or evidence to be used before any court, board, officer, or investigative committee.[6]

Types of Investigators

In order to understand who a private investigator is, it is important to distinguish between the different types of investigators in the legal system. Investigators fall into three broad categories: law enforcement, public, and private. Law enforcement investigators are sworn agents and employees of government agencies whose sole purpose is to enforce criminal statutes of the jurisdictions where they operate. Public investigators are employees of government agencies who provide criminal defense services or investigate specific regulatory or other non-criminal matters. In contrast, private investigators are licensed within a specific state or jurisdiction to work on behalf of private citizens, companies, or their legal counsel to investigate both criminal and civil matters. In this discussion we are going to focus solely on law enforcement and private investigators.

The primary role of law enforcement investigators is to enforce criminal laws on behalf of the citizenry within their respective jurisdictions. Although they may occasionally, with the permission of their agencies, work for private interests in a security function, they are first and foremost agents of state and county governments. Their ultimate goal is to make arrests based upon probable cause. Contrary to popular belief, the police do not actually represent the interests of victims, and they do not investigate matters of civil law, except in very rare instances, such as for civil seizures of the proceeds of crimes that they investigate. Within the scope of their purview, the police are required to enforce criminal laws in an equitable manner, conducting arrests and otherwise initiating investigations fairly and without prejudice, and based on the best interests of all citizens within their jurisdictions. They are also afforded powers that no other citizens have—including private investigators—to help them perform their obligations to enforce the laws, including applying for search warrants, seizing property, and making arrests.

In contrast to law enforcement, private investigators may not apply for search warrants, seize property, or make arrests, and the investigations they conduct are primarily, but not exclusively, regarding matters of civil law. The role of the private investigator in investigating crimes typically comes about while working on behalf of victims or for the defense of those accused of crimes. While private investigators do not have the same powers or often the monetary resources provided to law enforcement, they do have significant advantages. For example, they are not required to issue Miranda warnings prior to conducting interviews, and the goals of a private investigation may require a much lower level of evidentiary sufficiency than criminal convictions, the principle function of law enforcement.

With regard to the jurisdictions where a private investigator is authorized to work, private investigators are licensed by state, and most of the U.S. states and the District of Columbia require licensure. The licensing requirements for the various jurisdictions vary widely, and a small handful of states do not require an investigative license. For those states that do require licenses, however, the license only affords the investigator the authority to work within the confines of the licensing jurisdiction, except where some states with similar licensing requirements have engaged in multi-state **reciprocity agreements**, which empower investigators to legally enter other jurisdictions for brief periods of time and under limited circumstances. The agreements differ slightly by state but are fairly consistent overall. For example, in Virginia, which has limited reciprocity agreements with Florida, Louisiana, Georgia, North Carolina, Oklahoma, and Tennessee, the extra-jurisdictional investigations conducted in the other state are limited to cases that originate in the licensing state. Under the Virginia reciprocity agreements, all of the state agencies limit investigations conducted in their states to thirty days, except Tennessee, which limits investigations to fifteen days. When conducting an investigation in a reciprocating state, Virginia private investigators automatically consent to accept service of process for any legal matter arising out of the investigation through the Department of Criminal Justice Services (DCJS). This rule is intended to allow state courts, where citizens were harmed in some manner by investigators traveling to those states under reciprocity agreements, to continue exercising jurisdiction over those investigators for their harmful actions.

Some areas within states that have no state-level licensing requirements have local or country-level licensing requirements. Therefore, when operating in states without a state-licensing requirement, always check first with the county where you will be working.

The Law of the Private Investigation Profession

Except in the small handful of states where the practice of private investigation is not regulated, private investigators are defined by state statutes. The laws concerning the requirements to obtain a private investigator license vary widely from state to state, but they generally range from:

- States that do not have licensing or that have voluntary licensing
- States that only require background checks
- States that require background checks and some prior investigative experience
- States that require background checks, investigative experience, and an exam and/or training

The states that do not have licensing are Alabama, Alaska, Idaho, Mississippi, and South Dakota. Colorado was also in this category, but in 2012 they enacted voluntary licensing which requires the applicant to possess 4,000 hours of experience and undergo a background check. Note that even in states that do not require background checks, there are sometimes counties or cities within those states that require private investigators to be licensed in their jurisdictions. For example, the City of Fairbanks, Alaska requires private investigators to be licensed. The process, however, only involves paying a fee and undergoing a background check.

The next category includes those states and districts that only require applicants to pass a background check. These areas include Iowa, Kansas, New Hampshire, and Washington, D.C. What constitutes a criminal violation that will prohibit one from obtaining a license varies depending on the jurisdiction. However, provided one has a relatively clean record, it is possible to start a private investigations business with no experience in these locations. These areas, however, are the exception.

Most states—thirty-six jurisdictions, not including Colorado—require the principals of private investigation firms to also possess some level of experience, ranging from a year or less to five years. How these areas define relevant experience varies widely, but generally working as a private investigator or as a law enforcement investigator is suitable experience. Many areas also allow for partial waivers of experience if certain educational requirements are met, or if applicants complete an internship or other specialized training. Note that the experience requirements generally only apply to the principals of companies and not to the companies' employees, who in most instances do not need experience (although they may require training).

Sixteen states require private investigators to pass an exam. Six states also require the principals of companies to undergo training. Those states are Florida, Kentucky, Louisiana, Texas, Virginia, and Vermont.

Below is a summary of the licensing requirements for all fifty states and Washington, D.C.

Alabama
License required: No
Background check: N/A
Training required: N/A
Exam required: N/A
Investigative experience required: N/A

Alaska
License required: No
Background check: N/A
Training required: N/A
Exam required: N/A
Investigative experience required: N/A

Arizona
License required: Yes
Background check: Yes
Training required: No
Exam required: No
Investigative experience required: 3 years or prior law enforcement with experience in investigation

Arkansas
License required: Yes
Background check: Yes
Training required: No
Exam required: No
Investigative experience required: 2 years

California
License required: Yes
Background check: Yes
Training required: No
Exam required: 2-hour multiple choice exam
Investigative experience required: 3 years at 2,000 hours each year
  (can substitute some experience for a degree in criminal justice,
  political science, or related field)

Colorado
License required: Voluntary
Background check: Voluntary
Training required: N/A
Exam required: N/A
Investigative experience required: 4,000 hours or 2,000 hours plus
  a college degree; 400 hours can be earned through an approved
  investigative course

Connecticut
License required: Yes
Background check: Yes
Training required: Can substitute 1 year experience for training course
Exam required: No
Investigative experience required: 5 years or 10 years as police officer

Delaware
License required: Yes
Background check: Yes
Training required: No
Exam required: No
Investigative experience required: 5 years or former law enforcement
  who graduated from certified law enforcement academy

District of Columbia
License required: Yes
Background check: Yes
Training required: No
Exam required: No
Investigative experience required: No

Florida

License required: Yes
Background check: Yes
Training required: 40 hours for intern license (Class CC)
Exam required: Yes
Investigative experience required: 2 years for full license (Class C)

Georgia

License required: Yes
Background check: Yes
Training required: No
Exam required: No
Investigative experience required: 2 years or a 4-year degree in criminal justice or related field

Hawaii

License required: Yes
Background check: Yes
Training required: No
Exam required: Yes
Investigative experience required: 4 years

Idaho

License required: No
Background check: N/A
Training required: N/A
Exam required: N/A
Investigative experience required: N/A

Illinois

License required: Yes
Background check: Yes
Training required: No
Exam required: Yes
Investigative experience required: 3 years during last 5 years (a bachelor's degree in law enforcement or a related field or business can count toward 2 years; an associate's degree can count toward 1 year)

Indiana
License required: Yes
Background check: Yes
Training required: No
Exam required: No
Investigative experience required: 4,000 hours/2 years, or bachelor's degree in criminal justice or related field

Iowa
License required: Yes
Background check: Yes
Training required No
Exam required: No
Investigative experience required: No

Kansas
License required: Yes
Background check: Yes
Training required: No
Exam required: No
Investigative experience required: No

Kentucky
License required: Yes
Background check: Yes
Training required: Forty hours, six hours annual CPE
Exam required: Yes
Investigative experience required: No

Louisiana
License required: Yes
Background check: Yes
Training required: 40 hours
Exam required: Yes
Investigative experience required: 3 years within last 10 years

Maine

License required: Yes
Background check: Yes
Training required: No
Exam required: No
Investigative experience required: 3 years or a combination of experience, education, and sponsorship

Maryland

License required: Yes
Background check: Yes
Training required: No
Exam required: No
Investigative experience required: 5 years or 3 years supervisory experience

Massachusetts

License required: Yes
Background check: Yes
Training required: No
Exam required: No
Investigative experience required: 3 years, or 10 years if patrolman

Michigan

License required: Yes
Background check: Yes
Training required: No
Exam required: No
Investigative experience required: 3 years

Minnesota

License required: Yes
Background check: Yes
Training required: No
Exam required: No
Investigative experience required: 6,000 hours

Mississippi
License required: No
Background check: N/A
Training required: N/A
Exam required: N/A
Investigative experience required: N/A

Missouri
License required: Yes
Background check: Yes
Training required: No
Exam required: Yes
Investigative experience required: No

Montana
License required: Yes
Background check: Yes
Training required: No
Exam required: Yes
Investigative experience required: 3 years

Nebraska
License required: Yes
Background check: Yes
Training required: No
Exam required: Yes
Investigative experience required: 3,000 hours; or 2,500 hours with
    associate degree in field; or 2,000 hours with bachelor's degree

Nevada
License required: Yes
Background check: Yes
Training required: No
Exam required: Yes
Investigative experience required: 5 years, but with some credit given
    for certain education

New Hampshire
License required: Yes
Background check: Yes
Training required: No
Exam required: No
Investigative experience required: No

New Jersey
License required: Yes
Background check: Yes
Training required: No
Exam required: No
Investigative experience required: 5 years

New Mexico
License required: Yes
Background check: Yes
Training required: Certain continuing education requirements
Exam required: No
Investigative experience required: 6,000 hours within 5 years

New York
License required: Yes
Background check: Yes
Training required: No
Exam required: Yes
Investigative experience required: 3 years

North Carolina
License required: Yes
Background check: Yes
Training required: No
Exam required: No
Investigative experience required: 3 years

North Dakota
License required: Yes
Background check: Yes
Training required: No
Exam required: Yes
Investigative experience required: 2,000 hours

Ohio
License required: Yes
Background check: Yes
Training required: No
Exam required: Yes
Investigative experience required: 2 years

Oklahoma
License required: Yes
Background check: Yes
Training required: Yes, but only required if no experience
Exam required: Yes, but only required if no experience
Investigative experience required: 1 of last 3 years

Oregon
License required: Yes
Background check: Yes
Training required: No
Exam required: Yes
Investigative experience required: 1,500 hours

Pennsylvania
License required: Yes
Background check: Yes
Training required: No
Exam required: No
Investigative experience required: 3 years

Rhode Island

License required: Yes
Background check: Yes
Training required: No
Exam required: No
Investigative experience required: 5 years or degree in criminal justice

South Carolina

License required: Yes
Background check: Yes
Training required: Yes
Exam required: No
Investigative experience required: 3 years

South Dakota

License required: No
Background check: N/A
Training required: N/A
Exam required: N/A
Investigative experience required: N/A

Tennessee

License required: Yes
Background check: Yes
Training required: No
Exam required: No
Investigative experience required: 2,000 hours

Texas

License required: Yes
Background check: Yes
Training required: 40 hours
Exam required: Yes
Investigative experience required: 3 years; or a certain combination of education and experience; or completion of 200-hour course tailored to licensure

Utah
License required: Yes
Background check: Yes
Training required: No
Exam required: No
Investigative experience required: 2,000 hours for registrants, additional 8,000 hours for principal

Vermont
License required: Yes
Background check: Yes
Training required: 40 hours
Exam required: Yes
Investigative experience required: 2,000 hours during last 3 years

Virginia
License required: Yes
Background check: Yes
Training required: 60 hours, plus 8 hours of in-service for 2 years
Exam required: Yes
Investigative experience required: 5 years or 3 years supervising investigations

Washington
License required: Yes
Background check: Yes
Training required: No
Exam required: Yes, if less than 3 years' experience
Investigative experience required: 3 years, otherwise must take exam

West Virginia
License required: Yes
Background check: Yes
Training required: No
Exam required: No
Investigative experience required: 32 hours for 100 weeks (can substitute some or all experience for criminal justice degree or related education)

Wisconsin
License required: Yes
Background check: Yes
Training required: No
Exam required: 45 questions
Investigative experience required: No

Wyoming
License required: No
Background check: N/A
Training required: N/A
Exam required: N/A
Investigative experience required: N/A

As you can see from the summary provided, the laws vary widely from one state to the next. Notice that among the states that require licensing, it is common for the laws to require private investigation companies to have liability insurance and/or a bond, as well as a designated in-state registered agent. The state with the most stringent licensing laws is Virginia because its experience requirement is at the high end of all states (comparable with Connecticut, Delaware, Maryland, Nevada, and New Jersey), and its training requirement is the highest at sixty hours.[7] We will next examine Virginia licensing requirements in greater detail.

Case Study: Virginia

The profession of private investigation in Virginia is governed by two sources of law: (1) the Code of Virginia; and (2) the Regulations Related to Private Security Services promulgated under that statutory authority. The Code of Virginia provides the statutory laws that govern the regulation of private investigators and other private security categories. Among other provisions, the Code creates an administrative agency, the Department of Criminal Justice Services (DCJS), and authorizes it to issue regulations implementing the statute and the power to enforce those regulations. Because the DCJS's regulations both mirror the statute and then extrapolate upon the code, it is easiest from an educational standpoint to study the regulations.

Because the DCJS, the sole government entity that regulates private security services in Virginia, is relatively small—those tasked with investigating private security totaling only about four employees, who each must handle a caseload of forty to sixty complaints at any given time—its regulatory philosophy focuses primarily on investigative schools under their watch and on compliance agents, both tasked with furthering the compliance of private security businesses with applicable laws.[8] The idea is that directly policing thousands of security officers, bail bondsmen, and investigators is too difficult for a small group of people, but tasking a few hundred instructors and compliance agents with enforcing the regulations within their own purviews (i.e., within their classrooms and companies, respectfully) is more manageable. In this way, private security practitioners (private investigators included) are introduced to the regulations throughout their careers via the mandated entry-level and periodic in-service training, and are monitored internally at the companies where they work. It is not unusual for a private investigator registrant to never have any direct contact with the DCJS, except through their instructors and compliance agents. DCJS officials do periodically visit individual classes, however, mandating that all certified schools adhere to their regulations, which include using DCJS-approved course outlines and lesson plans consistent with the private security regulations. Similarly, they mandate record keeping policies for all licensed businesses and certified schools so as to better monitor compliance. For example, businesses must maintain employee records for three years after termination of employment.

Virginia Registration and Licensing Requirements

It is very important at the onset to note the distinction between private investigator registration and licensing. A private investigator is defined in the code and regulations as "any individual who engages in the business of, or accepts employment to make, investigations to obtain information on crimes or civil wrongs; the location, disposition, or recovery of stolen property; the cause of accidents, fires, damages, or injuries to persons or to property; or evidence to be used before any court, board, officer, or investigative committee.."[9] Anyone performing the tasks implicit in this definition is required to maintain a valid registration *and* to work for a licensed private security business authorized to conduct private investigations. There are some exceptions to the registration requirements, including persons exclusively engaged in the business of obtaining credit information; attorneys or certified public accountants licensed in Virginia; claims adjusters and their agents; secret shoppers; those who conduct solely government background checks; and those who are obtaining the information exclusively for their own purposes, sometimes called "end users." These people and businesses are not required to have a private investigator registration within the purview of their work. However, anyone soliciting business as a private investigator must first obtain a private investigator license.

To obtain a private investigator license in Virginia, the business must employ a certified compliance agent with three years' managerial experience (or five years' overall experience in the field) and have successfully completed an eight-hour course taught by DCJS. The business must also have a surety bond in the amount of $100,000 or insurance in the amount of $100,000/$300,000 and a designated registered agent to accept service of process in Virginia. Insurance protects the company in the event they are sued for any reason, while a bond only protects the government from a lawsuit in the event that a plaintiff also names the licensing agency in the suit. For this reason, insurance is strongly preferable to a bond. The $100,000 amount is the maximum amount of protection for any single event, while the $300,000 is the amount of total protection for any number of events. Most knowledgeable business owners opt to get double or even triple the insurance coverage than afforded by these minimally mandated amounts. Even though a company has obtained a license to operate a private investigative business, all persons engaged in investigative work for that company must be properly registered private investigators. Thus it is not permitted for licensed business with no registered investigators to actually conduct investigations, nor for a registered investigator with no license to operate a business independently. In other words, licenses and registrations are two distinct things—and both are required for a private investigative business to function within the law.

All applicants for private investigator registration must successfully complete the mandated sixty hours of training[10] The registration procedures and requirements also mandate successful completion of eight-hours of in-service training at a certified school every two years. Applicants must submit their fingerprints and an application fee of $25. There is also a fingerprint processing fee of $50. Licenses and registrations must be renewed every two years with the DCJS. While DCJS typically notifies registrants of the impending need for renewal, they are not required to do so. It is therefore recommended that investigators keep track of when their registrations are scheduled to expire and to prepare accordingly.

All of the courses certified by DCJS must meet the **compulsory minimum training requirements** as detailed in the regulations. These requirements specify a six-hour orientation, which includes the applicable sections of the laws and regulations, standards of professional conduct, and ethics; sixteen hours on criminal and civil law, including due process and privacy requirements; sixteen hours on basic investigative skills, including surveillance, research, and interviewing; eight hours on proper documentation, such as report writing, photography, audio recording, and testimony; and fourteen hours on various types of investigations, such as fraud, insurance, missing persons, and insurance investigations. There is also a required exam, which applicants must pass with a minimum score of seventy percent, and practical exercises, both of which are not included in the required sixty hours of class time.

Virginia Standards of Practice and Prohibited Acts

The regulations also specify several standards of practice and prohibited acts. These are the codified regulations that specify what private investigative businesses and registrants are prohibited from doing, and what they must do in compliance with the law. Notice that, while many of these regulations mimic some of the ethical issues discussed later (e.g., not representing oneself as a police officer), and others are similar to fairly well-known laws that apply to everyone in the Commonwealth and most other states, many of the standards below are purely regulatory in nature and are highly specific to our industry. These standards include, but are not exclusive to, the following:

- Maintaining at all times with DCJS a valid mailing address, email address, and phone number; and notifying DCJS in writing no later than ten days after the date of any change
- Informing DCJS and your employer in writing within ten days after being convicted of, or pleading guilty to, any crime, or being found guilty of violating the private security services laws or regulations of any jurisdiction, not only Virginia
- Not being convicted of a felony or any crime involving moral turpitude

- Not soliciting, contracting to provide, or performing private investigative services without having a private security services business license
- Carrying a valid registration or valid temporary authorization letter at all times while on duty
- Possessing a valid firearms training endorsement while carrying a firearm during an investigation, and then only with a letter of authorization from the employer's compliance agent
- Not representing oneself as a law-enforcement officer or other government official
- Displaying one's registration while on duty in response to the request of a law-enforcement officer, DCJS personnel, or client
- Not providing information obtained by the registrant or his employing firm to any person other than the client who secured the services of the licensee without the client's prior written consent, except as otherwise provided by law
- Not making any misrepresentation to a client
- Satisfying all judgments related to private security services not provided[11]

Although there are more standards of practice than mentioned above, these are the standards most applicable to private investigator registrants, such as keeping the DCJS and one's employer abreast of your contact information and any criminal convictions; upholding the confidentiality of case information; and maintaining proper documentation for one's registrations and authorization to carry firearms. The standards pertaining to carrying firearms in our profession deserve special mention, because, although Virginia is a so-called "right to carry" state with regard to the issuance of concealed handgun permits,[12] private investigators who carry a handgun concealed, or who otherwise have access to a firearm while on duty, must have received a firearms endorsement from the DCJS. The investigator must also have the explicit permission from her employer's compliance agent. This letter of authorization must then be kept with her at all times while she is in possession of a firearm, concealed or not, while she is on the clock.

DCJS may demand, and in some cases subpoena, records necessary for their investigation of a complaint. Once the matter has been investigated and thoroughly adjudicated, remedial actions can include license revocation and fines up to $2,500 per offense. Violations of many of the statutes also constitute Class Two misdemeanors and can be referred to the Office of the Commonwealth Attorney for criminal prosecution. During 2008, there were 654 complaints about private security businesses in Virginia, of which fifty-eight percent were determined to be founded, generating over $91,000 in fines.[13] Most of the founded cases (twenty-six percent) involved complaints of unlicensed activity. All penalties are given to the State Literary Fund. DCJS may also seek to recover costs of their investigation from the offending entity.[14] This is all to say that the DCJS takes its mandate to enforce the rules very seriously.

> **Discussion:** *Which states currently do not have private investigation licensing requirements? Which states require applicants to undergo investigative training? Which states currently have reciprocity agreements with the Commonwealth of Virginia? What is the purpose of reciprocity agreements and why are they important? Why do you think that Virginia does not have similar agreements with other states? What is the compulsory minimum amount of hours that student investigators must study the law and documentation during the 02E course? Why do the regulations place such a large emphasis on the law for private investigators?*

2

The Ethics of Being a
Private Investigator

As a private investigator, you will certainly be called upon to examine your ethics in light of circumstances that arise during investigations. One reason why conducting investigations in the private sector is so fraught with ethical dilemmas is because the interests of our private clients sometimes do not coincide with the broader interests of society, or with the interests of the opposing parties in adverse litigation. As private investigators, we are tasked with conducting investigations in furtherance of a particular private interest, but this does not discharge us from the responsibility that we also have as citizens to not harm other citizens. According to an article in *Smart Money*, frequent complaints from the public about private investigators include that they:

- Work for unsavory persons, who then break the law with the information provided by the investigator;
- Use unethical and illegal practices while gathering information;
- Mislead clients or do not fully inform them about what an investigation will entail.[15]

Although some of the claims in the article may be exaggerated, they raise very legitimate concerns, considering the uniquely independent and powerful role that private investigators have in our society.

Ethical Foundations

Due to the frequency of ethical questions, it is imperative that private investigators have an understanding of the foundation on which their own principles are grounded. The most basic ethical principle is the **imperative principle**, which requires a decision maker to act according to an ethical rule. That rule may be as simple as "do not steal." The imperative principle is most applicable when circumstances are very carefully described or codified, as with laws (e.g., perjury) or established mores. **Mores** are social norms or practices particular to a given culture. In America, an example of a *mos* is the common practice of shaking an outstretched hand.[16] Since decidedly *not* shaking someone's hand when he has offered it is perceived as an affront in American society, this may also be an example of a moral imperative.

The imperative principle is highly applicable as a private investigator, as it is essential for investigators to have an established set of moral imperatives that define what they will absolutely not do during an investigation. In other words, by knowing that it is never okay to steal an item that belongs to another person, an investigator will be cognizant of avoiding tactics that include this behavior. In this way, an investigator will be less likely to rationalize questionable behavior in the middle of an investigation, thereby violating her established ethical principles. Likewise, knowledge of social mores existing in United States and other cultures is important, too, because these common practices make up the unwritten fabric of ethical societal relations. For example, some Muslim cultures prescribe that women cover their hair with a hijab in public. While Americans may believe this practice is sexist, it nonetheless represents a social custom that must be respected when conducting investigations in cultures where that practice is observed.

> **Discussion:** How might you apply the imperative principle in your personal or professional life? For example, is it ever okay to lie (e.g., during an undercover investigation)? Is it ever okay to steal (e.g., if your family is starving)? What are some American societal mores that might also represent moral imperatives?

Another ethical ideal, the **utilitarian principle**, maintains that the ultimate criterion of an ethical decision is the balance of positive consequences over negative consequences produced by an action. As investigators for private interests, it is helpful to keep in mind that the interests of our clients are not necessarily those that are best for society as a whole, and, in fact, the interests of clients can sometimes be completely contrary to society's interests. However, this dichotomy is generally acceptable—and indeed largely unavoidable in our profession—because "society" is really a conglomeration of a myriad of private interests. It is widely acknowledged and accepted in capitalist societies that the collective of all private interests working on their own behalf, and regulated by society's laws and norms, is what allows society to function freely.

However, this is not to say that private interests exist completely independent of the society collective; rather, every private interest also has an obligation to play by the rules prescribed by the greater society and, at the end of the day, to contribute something positive to the whole. The utilitarian principle is useful to consider during private investigations because it puts this diversity of sometimes conflicting private interests in perspective. There is a point at which an investigator must ask if she is comfortable working on behalf of a private interest that may be detrimental to society. While most Americans would probably never willingly work directly for Osama Bin Laden, many investigators would feel comfortable working on behalf of the defense attorney for a person charged with acts of terrorism. The point at which an investigator will begin questioning her morals in light of the utilitarian principle differs with each individual. By remaining conscious of the positive contribution that her work affords society—and the ever-present risk of potentially negative contributions—an investigator will find it easier to achieve a sum-positive ethical balance.

> **Discussion:** *Who would you be uncomfortable working for? For example, would you work as a defense investigator for a child molester, assuming that you knew he probably committed the crime? Would you work for a toy manufacturer who was attempting to develop alternative theories related to severe injuries to children caused by its defective products? Use the utilitarian principle to determine how the private interests of these parties conflict with society's interests, and how these interests might converge with the collective interests of society?*

Professional Ethics Codes

Aside from personal ethical principles, which differ by individual and are necessarily shaped by one's cultural upbringing and experiences, well established, professional ethical codes related to the field of private investigation also exist, such as those set forth by professional investigative organizations. Most states, including Virginia, have state associations. The largest private investigation association in Virginia is the Private Investigators Association of Virginia (PIAVA).[17] The codes and statements of purpose for these private investigative associations can reveal a great deal about how the profession sees its place and responsibilities in relation to society. Taken from their website, **PIAVA's Code of Ethics** reads as follows:

- To conduct myself in my profession with honesty, sincerity, integrity, fidelity, morality, and good conscience in all dealings with my clients
- To preserve forever my clients' confidence under any and all circumstances and deal justly, and impartially with each individual, irrespective of social, political, racial, ethnic, or religious considerations, economic status, or physical characteristics
- To conduct all my investigations within the bounds of legality, morality, and professional ethics
- To council my clients against any illegal or unethical course of action
- To explain to the full satisfaction of my clients all fees and charges in their cases and to render factual reports
- To maintain my own professional reputation and that of my fellow investigators and professional associates
- To support to the best of my ability the professional goals of the Private Investigators Association of Virginia, Inc.
- To contribute to better community relations through work and deed to elevate the status of the investigative profession
- To ensure that all my employees adhere to this Code of Ethics

According to past-PIAVA President Edward Hruneni, the Association's Code of Ethics, written in 1982, was not intended to address any specific abuses in the industry; rather, it was written to provide guidelines for how "members should conduct themselves and their businesses in dealing with their clients" and to "promote a suggested professional, ethical standard for the industry."[18] This makes these guidelines significant, because, as the premiere private investigative association in Virginia, PIAVA and its Code of Ethics is the closest thing to a statewide industry consensus regarding what one can and cannot do as an investigator beyond mere codified laws. This is equally true of other states' private investigation associations' codes of ethics. For example, while satisfactorily explaining fees to clients is not a legal requirement, fair and proper time keeping and transparent billing practices are an important industry objective. Recall that a failure to fairly and fully inform clients about investigations is among the most common public complaints about private investigators. Although the codes of ethics of various state private investigation associations may not have been designed to remedy specific abuses, they were surely intended, at a minimum, to establish a baseline of ethical behavior among their members, so as to address such general areas of potential abuse.

> *Discussion: What benefit might there be for private investigators to participate in national and state private investigation associations? What does PIAVA's Code of Ethics tell someone who knows very little about private investigators? Does this message conflict with the image of private investigators in the media? If so, what are the possible reasons for this disparity between the way our industry sees itself and how the media sees us?*

Professionalism

In addition to understanding basic ethical principles and codes, private investigators should also understand how they fit into their chosen profession, and how their profession fits into society. This aspect of belonging to something bigger than oneself is sometimes referred to as **professionalism**. Much more than just aesthetics and etiquette—qualities important in their own right—professionalism involves acting as a member of a professional field. One quasi-investigative association, the Association of Certified Fraud Examiners (ACFE),[19] lists factors that differentiate professional fields, in their case, fraud examiners, from nonprofessional vocations, and they include:

- A body of specialized knowledge acquired by formal education
- Admission to the profession governed by standards of professional conduct
- Recognition and acceptance by society of professional status, and concurrent recognition and acceptance of social responsibility by the professional
- Standards of conduct governing relationships of the professional with clients, colleagues, and the public

- A national organization devoted to the advancement of the obligations of the professional group[20]

The concept of professionalism typically evokes thoughts of **behavioral mannerisms**, defined as an investigator's ability to abide by established societal mores. Behavioral mannerisms can differ markedly in various cultures and societal strata. Although many argue that these factors are fundamentally superficial, aesthetics and etiquette are incredibly important for success in our society, especially for investigators who are often tasked with gaining people's trust.

As a general rule, the more "formal" an investigator's appearance and behavior, within reasonable limits, the more she will be perceived as a professional, e.g., as someone who can be trusted with important information. However, behaving "formally" in an informal setting can also be problematic in many circumstances, such as in a more relaxed cultural environment or among younger people who tend to eschew formality in action and dress. Nevertheless, society is generally more forgiving of lapses in formality than in lapses in informality. Therefore, when in doubt, it is generally best to err on the side of being perceived as "too formal."

> **Discussion:** Discuss a time that when you or someone you know made an error in aesthetics or etiquette (e.g., wore something less than professional to a job interview, become too personal with a supervisor, etc.). What were the consequences of this error? Had the error not occurred, would anything have happened differently?

Another factor that differentiates professional groups from nonprofessional groups is a **formal education**, which can vary from a university degree to mandated training, such as the investigative training mandated in Florida, Kentucky, Louisiana, Texas, Virginia, and Vermont. While private investigators are generally not *required* to have college degrees (although some states count college degrees toward experience), they are generally required to have a substantial amount of knowledge about the law, criminology, and other subjects that certainly equate, at a minimum, to an undergraduate degree. Virginia, for example, recognizes this fact, which is why DCJS has mandated sixty hours as the minimum requirement—more than any other state—for those seeking to work as private investigators in the Commonwealth. However, this minimum requirement is not in itself enough to impart the degree of knowledge and expertise required to conduct most investigations. The only way to become an effective and successful investigator is by continually seeking opportunities for formal education to improve investigative skills, whether in surveillance, interviewing, or the like. Investigators must also continually read and study to remain current on the ever-changing laws directly affecting the profession, such as laws relating to privacy or governing access to particular types of information. Without formal education, an investigator will fall behind the professional curve, thereby doing her company, her clients, and herself a tremendous disservice.

We have already seen an example of professional standards in PIA-VA's Code of Ethics, but many other investigative associations have also established similar **professional standards** that shape the way the profession perceives its place in society. In addition to these codified standards, there are several other generally accepted, but often unwritten, standards governing our profession, such as properly vetting your clients, and not working for clients without adequate legal or similar justification. More than just general ethical guidelines, these standards are one of the factors that set investigators apart as members of a professional occupation—exactly *because* of our introspection and desire to have standards that help define us as a group. Members of professional occupations are concerned not only with their own individual wellbeing—because they identify closely with their collective occupation—but they are also greatly concerned about the standards of the group as a whole. This factor differentiates private investigators from construction workers or mechanics, for example, who are less concerned about the collective standards of their respective professions than with their personal and company standards.[21]

Discussion: Consider other professional occupations (e.g., accountants, lawyers, etc.). What formal educational requirements and professional standards govern these groups of professionals? How do these groups police their members to abide by their ethical and professional guidelines?

Another factor that differentiates professional occupations from nonprofessional occupations is **societal recognition**. Private investigators admittedly have had some difficulty in this area, primarily due to unflattering media portrayals, and the actions of some wayward investigators who have opted to eschew the collective professional standards and engage in unethical or unsavory behavior. One admittedly low point in our profession were the despicable actions of prominent Hollywood investigator Anthony Pellicano, who was convicted of seventy-eight different criminal charges, including wiretapping and racketeering in 2008.[22] This behavior reflects very poorly on the profession as a whole, and hurts us dearly with regard to achieving full-fledged societal recognition. Recall the earlier discussion of the utilitarian principle and how it is important to estimate how our actions might affect others in society. Recognition and acceptance by society as a professional occupation that values the rights and wellbeing of others is the flipside of this coin. As a whole, however, society *does* recognize the value and responsibility of our collective profession, as evidenced by the fact that we exist as a licensed entity in all but four states in the country. However, full-fledged societal recognition is the most lofty and important goal as a collective, because with it will come a more cohesive professional identity and undoubtedly greater access to information vital to investigations.

Aside from personal actions, the primary vehicle by which education, standards, and recognition are developed is via **professional associations**. There are over seventy-five state and national investigative associations, and their missions and scopes vary considerably. For example, there is the Association of Christian Investigators and the Korean-American Association of Licensed Detectives. These and similar groups, regardless of their specifically defined intent or purpose, serve to impart formal educational standards to all private investigators, develop generally agreed upon standards for the profession, and lobby on behalf of societal recognition. Professional associations are the hallmark of professional occupations. Without membership in such groups, there is little consensus as to what exactly a "private investigator" *is,* beyond the basic statutory definition and the responsibilities a person calling herself a "private investigator" has toward society under formally codified laws. For example, as Hruneni puts it, membership in the PIAVA is "a symbol of acceptance by peers in the industry, as well as a symbol of experience and integrity for potential clients."[23] In other words, membership in an association bestows professional belonging to an investigator, and signifies to the public that the member is a part of something bigger than herself.

Belonging to associations allows an investigator to have ready connections in jurisdictions where she is not otherwise licensed. The role of investigators as a whole has increasingly become more international during the past decade, primarily due to the prevalence of the Internet and globalization. The profession has thereby become more global in scope, and it is therefore essential to have resources beyond our immediate national and international borders. National groups, such as the National Association of Legal Investigators (NALI) and the National Council on Investigative and Security Specialists (NCISS), and international groups, such as the Counsel of International Investigators (CII) and the World Association of Detectives (WAD), can greatly assist extrajurisdictional investigations, because their members, respectively, originate from virtually all parts of the Unites States and the world.[24]

Discussion: What other professional groups have difficulty achieving societal recognition? Why? What other professional associations have you heard of or do you belong to? What sorts of activities do these groups provide for their members? Why might it be helpful, or even important, to belong to such groups?

Misrepresentation and Bias

After examining basic ethical principles and our profession as a collective, it is important to next review the most prevalent ethical and professional dilemmas that arise in private investigations, and to establish a framework that will hopefully be useful in guiding subsequent decisions. Two very common problems are **misrepresentation** and **bias**. A private investigator must never misrepresent the truth in any investigative report or during testimony, and must never allow her personal biases to sway her judgment during an investigation. Bluntly put, these are moral imperatives. The problem arises when investigators become too close to one side of a dispute or do not recognize and account for their inherent biases. The issue of whether one can ever be truly objective is an ancient philosophical conundrum that is outside the scope of this text. However, there are two common factors that can often cause an investigator to inadvertently (and occasionally *advertently*) misrepresent facts during an investigation.

The first is racism and other prejudgments; essentially believing that one group of people is inferior in some quality, and allowing this fundamental assumption to shape all interactions or experiences with members of this group. Keep in mind that these beliefs can be engrained to the point that we do not realize we have them. This bias becomes a self-fulfilling prophecy and leads an investigator to make basic factual misjudgments that can skew the results of an investigation to support the underlying bias. While this may seem like an obvious pitfall to avoid, too often underlying biases become disguised as basic assumptions that we take for granted. Prejudice also need not be as blatant as racial or sexual bias; anytime an investigator prejudges the facts before they are uncovered, or otherwise relies wholly on inductive reasoning to reach an investigative conclusion, the results are necessarily suspect. It is therefore prudent to know one's own prejudices and to adequately adjust for them before undertaking an investigation.

The second major pitfall encountered in the profession is that of partisanship, or aligning oneself too closely with the positions of clients. The role of an investigator is to be an objective fact finder. The issue of whether one can ever be truly objective is highly debatable, but the tendency to assume the position of the person paying the bill is so engrained and common in our field that it demands special focus. Many investigators find themselves gravitating toward clients and cases that appeal to their societal orientation, such as assisting the perceived downtrodden or helping big businesses function correctly. To a large extent, this is normal. However, it is essential that investigators avoid becoming pawns to the causes of their clients. This is accomplished by maintaining one's professional identity and avoiding personal or political relationships with our clientele. Recall the utilitarian principle.

Discussion: Discuss a time when you or someone you know became too close to an issue, thereby affecting judgment. How might you have acted otherwise, had you remained objective and impartial to the situation?

Honesty

To take the problem of misrepresentation and bias a little further, a private investigator must never misrepresent the truth in any investigative report or during testimony. This, too, is a moral imperative. While it is okay generally to misrepresent the truth at certain times during an interrogation or during an undercover investigation—with some very important exceptions discussed later—dishonesty has no place once a case has entered the legal system, or in dealings with clients or the government. The rule is that, aside from the very limited circumstances where misrepresenting the truth is warranted, an investigator should always tell the truth, no matter how inconvenient it may be to the underlying investigation. While this may seem like a given, there is often enormous pressure to bend the truth to make the client happier—because happy clients make *repeat* clients. However, an investigator should never fall into this trap because she will inevitably be discovered and exposed when she is called to testify, assuming, of course, that she does not take the lie a step further and opt to commit perjury—thereby becoming a felon. In short, nobody will want to hire an investigator who has lost her credibility.

Any discussion about honesty in our field should also refer to the point at which we "join" the profession by becoming registered private investigators through our respective states, and when we undergo the process (as licensed businesses) of soliciting clients to use our services. Most, if not all, of the states that have private investigation licensing provisions require applicants to tell the truth during the application process. In Virginia, for example, all applicants are expressly prohibited from engaging in any fraud or omission on their applications for their registration applications or renewals.[25] Likewise, private security registrants, businesses, and schools are prohibited from publishing any written business advertisements or material that is false or misleading, or from making misrepresentations to clients or potential clients.[26] Dishonesty with regard to credentials or in advertisements to the public can be the grounds for losing one's registration (and license or certification, if applicable) and possible criminal prosecution.

Perjury is viewed as such a heinous crime in our society by those that are familiar with our legal system, because our court system, and by extension the entire apparatus by which legal grievances are addressed and remedied in our country, is dependent on truth telling. While judges and jurors do make determinations about the veracity of testimony, they largely take witnesses at their word. Therefore, a person who commits perjury, be it through evasion or omission of facts or outright deception, is circumventing this fundamental process at its core. This may seem like an obvious point, but there are several noteworthy differences between investigators and others who may be called to testify as witnesses. First, as investigators, we are typically paid by one party to the dispute, and therefore have a built-in incentive to assist our client, possibly providing a motive to lie. Secondly, because of our role as fact finders, we are aware long before the average witness that the steps we take during an investigation are likely to be the subject of testimony at some time in the future. Essentially, we are *preparing* to testify from the moment we begin an investigation. As such, we should never do or say anything during an investigation that we would ultimately be uncomfortable testifying to under oath and under penalty of perjury in a court of law. In other words, an investigator should treat the entire investigation as if she will have to testify about it later.

> **Discussion:** *Has there ever been a time when you felt pressure to lie but ultimately decided to tell the truth? What motivated you to tell the truth? What were the consequences of your truth telling? What would have happened differently, had you chosen not to tell the truth?*

Conflicts of Interest

Conflicts of interest, defined as a real or *seeming* incompatibility between a private interest and an investigator's public responsibilities, constitute another major problem for private investigators. The operative word in the above definition is "seeming," meaning that anytime there is even the appearance of a conflict of interest—then it is, by definition, a conflict of interest. Conflicts of interest can include personal or professional affiliations with an adverse party in the dispute at issue, or with a co-defendant, co-plaintiff, or other party in a lawsuit. This does not necessarily mean the investigator is precluded from working on the case, but it does require objectivity and complete honesty about the nature of the conflict. When presented with a potential conflict while working on a client's case, the investigator must disclose the conflict to the relevant parties and allow them to make the decision as to whether it presents a situation where she should bow out of the investigation. Such issues may sometimes be overcome by full disclosure and universal agreement of all parties that the conflict should be waived.

Confidentiality

Because private investigators are frequently used in court cases where the personal or financial stakes are high, confidentiality is also a mainstay of our profession. It often goes without saying that our investigations are "confidential," although not many people stop to think what this actually means. Essentially, we are strictly forbidden to discuss our investigations, except with our clients or those immediately involved in the case at hand, and when otherwise required by law. While it may be tempting to brag about a particularly interesting case to your spouse or colleague over a drink, this is considered unethical and may in some instances be illegal. The Virginia regulations specify that private security businesses are not to provide any information obtained by the firm or its agents to anyone other than the client, without the client's prior written consent.[27] This broad requirement does not apply to information officially requested through the courts or through law enforcement agencies, such as with a subpoena. It is therefore prudent to view strict confidentiality as a moral imperative with a few, narrow exceptions, primarily those involving official governmental requests regarding criminal investigations or when under subpoena.

Strictly speaking, there is no legal privilege protecting information shared between a private investigator and her client, although the attorney-client privilege that attorneys have may be extended to private investigators working as agents of attorneys. This means that private investigators may be legally compelled to disclose confidential information pertaining to their clients in the event they are not working through an attorney. Of course, this is a very good reason why an investigator should always choose from the beginning to work under the auspices of an attorney, if possible.

Sound Business Practices

Having established practices in place as a matter of routine business is critical in avoiding costly legal and ethical dilemmas. This is sometimes referred to as **sound business practices**, and it essentially involves having procedures and practices in place before a problem occurs—not afterward. Sound business practices include having contracts for all business relationships related to an investigation, and maintaining appropriate notes and documentation for all work performed. As we discuss the methods of investigation later in the text, it is prudent to keep in mind that these are all sound business practices specific to our field that are designed to avoid common pitfalls. Just because a certain method is the fastest or most efficient manner of performing a given task does not mean that it is the *best* method. For example, it may be more time efficient to forego a lengthy written report and simply call the client and tell them the results of your investigation. However, in the long run it is better to have established methods or patterns of performing similar tasks, such as writing investigative reports, in order to nullify allegations of inadequacy, bias, etc.—because the investigator has performed the same task in the same manner in the dozen instances before and after the task at issue.

A specific example of a sound business practice that addresses a common problem encountered while conducting investigations is the way in which an investigator identifies herself. Allegations that private investigators misrepresent themselves as agents of law enforcement are common in our industry. This is not necessarily because there are a lot of private investigators claiming to be police officers, however. The allegations usually stem from a public misunderstanding of what private investigators actually do. When a citizen encounters an "investigator," but has never encountered a *private* investigator before, and has an ill-informed notion of what a private investigator actually looks like, he oftentimes assumes that the investigator before him is a police officer. When the citizen later learns that his assumption was incorrect, he will often complain that he was misled by the investigator. One way to counter these types of complaints is for an investigator to always introduce herself the same way every time she encounters a witness. For example, she might say, "My name is Sarah Mitchell, and I am a private investigator for Dinolt Becnel & Wells Investigative Group LLC, working on behalf of the ABC Insurance Company." In this example, the name of the client (e.g., the ABC Insurance Company) will differ in every case, but the investigator otherwise will not alter the other elements of her stock introduction. Using the same introduction in every instance is a sound business practice because it limits the potential for misunderstandings. The investigator will also have a ready, more-credible reply regarding how she has introduced herself, should such an allegation ever arise.

> **Discussion:** *What are examples of other sound business practices that you have encountered in your career? Do sound business practices ever impede the efficiency of daily operations? Discuss a specific time when a sound business practice, previously taken for granted, turned out to save you or your employer from a major problem.*

Conclusion

Part I addressed the differences between private and public investigators, and summarized the licensing laws in all fifty states plus Washington, D.C. It then detailed the laws in the jurisdiction with the most stringent licensing requirements for private investigators: Virginia. Understanding these laws is critical to our profession, because they allow us to operate as investigators in the areas where we are licensed.

Part I also discussed many of the ethical issues that are prevalent in our industry, and broached the topic of professionalism and professional conduct. Professional consciousness is essential to remain firmly grounded in a profession that is fraught with moral pitfalls. A belief in the ties that unite us, and a thorough understanding of the laws that regulate us as a group, is necessary to become a private investigator. This is so because being a private investigator is much more than falling under its statutory definition; it is belonging to a powerful and dignified collective occupation, and making sound ethical decisions informed both by healthy introspection and by the ethical codes of relevant professional associations. Being a private investigator means knowing and adhering to the regulations and to the law, not only being an expert in the practice of conducting investigations, which only comes *after* a firm grasp of the rules of the game, so to speak. In Part II, we will discuss the nuts and bolts of conducting investigations in the private sector.

Notes

1. Becnel, P.A. (2012). *Principles of Investigative Documentation*. Charles C. Thomas Publishing Ltd.: Chicago.

2. For my first few classes I used *Internal Investigations in the Workplace* by Eugene Ferraro, published by Auesbach Publications in 2006. Ferraro's book thoroughly teaches how to conduct internal investigations, but its limited scope ultimately makes it inadequate for teaching an entry-level private investigator course.

3. In some respects, this work has represented a crossover from investigating to consulting, as I now spend a good amount of my time working for plaintiff lawyers to interview their clients and ascertain whether they are being truthful or deceptive about their claims. In other words, since I offer my expert opinion in this service, I am no longer just a neutral fact finder.

4. Regulations Related to Private Security Services 6 VAC 20-171-230 and 6 VAC 20-171-320

5. Regulations Related to Private Security Services 6 VAC 20-171-300

6. Code of Virginia § 9.1 – 138

7. For full disclosure, I am the President of the Private Investigators Association of Virginia as I write this. Also, Puerto Rico, a U.S. territory, happens to have more stringent licensing laws than Virginia. Puerto Rico requires its private investigators to undergo 1,080 hours of training, unless they have eight years' law enforcement experience.

8. Since I wrote this, DCJS underwent a reorganization that eliminated its Private Security Section and incorporated the private security regulatory function into the sections dealing broadly with enforcement and training. Despite these changes, however, their philosophy has not changed, save perhaps for a greater focus on proactive enforcement.

9. Code of Virginia § 9.1-138 and Regulations Relating to Private Security Services 6 VAC 20-171-10

10. In some instances, persons with certain law enforcement experience may waive parts of the required training with DCJS approval, as per the Regulations Related to Private Security Services 6 VAC 20-171-445 and 6 VAC 10-171-450.

11. Regulations Related to Private Security 6 VAC 20-171-230 and 6 VAC 20-171-320

12. Code of Virginia §18.2-308

13. I obtained these statistics from a DCJS investigator during my in-service compliance agent training in 2008.

14. Regulations Related to Private Security Services 6 VAC 20-171-480 through 6 VAC 20-171-560

15. Motia, Shahryar. "10 things Your Private Investigator Won't Tell You." *Smart Money*. 10/08.

16. The term "mores" does not have a singular form in English. The Latin word is the plural form of "mos," which is not commonly used in English, but which I use in this text to demonstrate my point.

17. For more information about joining the PIAVA, visit www.piava.org.

18. Hruneni, Edward. Personal email correspondence dated 02/02/09.

19. For more information about joining the ACFE, visit www.afce.com.

20. Wells, Joseph, et al. (2005). *Fraud Examiners Manual*. Association of Certified Fraud Examiners: 4.902.

21. This is not to write disparagingly about construction workers or mechanics. As someone who worked as both a carpenter's helper and a motorcycle mechanic, I know these jobs require a tremendous amount of physical skill and mental know-how. Still, in my nearly four years cleaning carburetors and rebuilding motorcycle engines,

not once did I wax about the epistemology of these tasks with my fellow mechanics, despite what Robert M. Pirsig's *Zen and the Art of Motorcycle Maintenance* might imply.

22. Kravitz, Derek. "Sleuth to the Stars Gets 15-Year Sentence." *The Washington Post* online. 12/16/08.

23. Hruneni, Edward. Personal email correspondence dated 02/02/09.

24. Information about joining these associations may be obtained from their websites, respectively: www.nalionlin.org, www.nciss.org, www.cii2.org, and www.wad.net.

25. Regulations Related to Private Security Services 6 VAC 20-171-320

26. Regulations Related to Private Security Services 6 VAC 20-171-230

27. Regulations Related to Private Security Services 6 VAC 20-171-230 and 6 VAC 20-171-320

Part II
Investigative Skills

3

The Scientific Method

The underlying goal of every investigation is to gather and document evidence in a manner that will be admissible in a subsequent court proceeding, such that—when it is viewed by a reasonable person with no knowledge of the matter under investigation—it will tend to prove or disprove some material element of the disputed event. Since it is often difficult to determine what given fact is going to be material at the conclusion of an investigation, it is critical to document *all* evidence uncovered during an investigation as if it were of equal importance. An investigation is an attempt to establish the likely cause of some event, similar to a scientific experiment that might, for example, try to determine the cause of some natural phenomenon (e.g., gravity). The methods used by scientists to determine cause and effect are equally applicable to an investigation. Scientists call this unknown link between cause and effect the "problem," as in a mathematical equation. Whether investigators term their system of investigation the "scientific method," the "component method"[1] or some other name, every investigation begins with a clear understanding of what problem needs to be solved, and every investigator employs logical reasoning to systematically uncover and test possible solutions to that problem.

The first step in any investigation is to clearly **state the problem**. The problem of a case is more than the obvious elements of a dispute, such as one person's word against another. More significantly, the problem includes the overarching goal of the investigation: the desired outcome of the case. In other words, it is not enough to state, for example, that the problem is to identify the suspect in a store theft; the problem also includes the best means of clearly establishing that the suspect did, in fact, steal the merchandise. It also includes gathering admissible evidence. Another important component of the problem in the private sector is working within the budgetary requirements of the case. Recall that private investigation is a profit-oriented endeavor. Our clients' budgets therefore largely define the scope of our investigations. It is imperative that the investigator know and be able to articulate the problem as it relates to evidentiary goals and any budget restraints before beginning the investigation. A failure to state the problem results in unnecessary investigative work, missed benchmarks, and unhappy clients.

The next step is to **form the hypothesis**, which is the theory or theories that guide the investigation. In an investigation concerning litigation, the hypothesis is likely to be determined by whatever the plaintiff or defendant (whoever hired the investigator) says occurred. During an internal investigation, the hypothesis will likely be influenced by the investigator's experience conducting similar investigations and by the probable opportunity and motives of suspects. Beware, however, that forming a broad hypothesis based on limited facts is an exclusively deductive method of reasoning, by definition. This can create a myopic vision of reality if an investigator adheres to a hypothesis that does not make sense in light of the evidence. The hypothesis can therefore change several times during the course of an investigation, as the investigator discovers, for example, that another hypothesis answers the problem better than the first one. Testing the hypothesis involves **observation and experimentation**. The typical tools and techniques useful for testing a hypothesis are research, interviews, and surveillance. Each of these fact-gathering techniques will be discussed in great detail later in this section.

After thorough observation and experimentation, the investigator must **interpret the data** uncovered during the investigation. Finding evidence is not the most difficult part of most investigations; documenting and analyzing evidence that is relevant to an investigation often proves to be the most trying task. It is for this reason that the time spent preparing investigative reports typically takes about double the time spent actually conducting an investigation. This phase takes excellent organizational and communication skills. Some analytical investigative software programs can greatly assist in the analysis of complex investigative data. After collecting the evidence in the observation and experimentation phase of the investigation, the investigator should set aside (but not discard) evidence that is not material to solving the investigation's stated problem. The remaining evidence, whether it supports the hypothesis or not, should then be carefully documented, logically organized, and closely analyzed to determine what it tells the investigator about the validity of the hypothesis. The methods of investigative documentation will be discussed in Part III.

Once the evidence has been gathered and documented, the final step it to **draw conclusions**. Do the facts support or refute the hypothesis? If the former, then the investigator should carefully document the findings, investigate any loose ends not covered during the observation and experimentation phase, and submit a final report detailing the solution of the problem. Depending on the type of case and the interpretation of the information uncovered, it may be necessary to revisit and restate the hypothesis several times before the case can be concluded with confidence that the problem has been satisfied above the applicable level of evidence sufficiency (e.g., clear and convincing evidence). Note that "drawing conclusions" is not the same as judging guilt or innocence. An investigator should never offer a judgment or opinion during an investigation. The investigator's job is exclusively to report facts or evidence and to properly qualify the findings, such that she does not become partisan to the client's personal or legal goals.

Discussion: What are the five steps of the scientific method? Name a few investigations that you have recently heard about in the news, and clearly state the problem of each case. Using the scientific method as a roadmap, how might these cases be investigated in light of the stated problem? Could these cases be investigated differently if the problem was defined differently or remained undefined?

4

Research

The universe of information available to investigators is so large, and the methods of obtaining it so varied, that it is exceedingly difficult to categorize types of information or to discuss the methods of conducting research in any reasoned way. Research is more art than science, and obtaining information from third-party sources is typically accomplished through significant trial and error. Even when an investigator finally learns the ins and outs of navigating an informational system, often the system changes in some manner, requiring her to learn the system anew. For example, an investigator who frequently works criminal cases filed in a particular courthouse may know the court clerk and many of the local police officers on a first-name basis, but as those people move on to other jobs and the like, the system changes and she has to learn the means of accessing information all over again. In other words, any book that purports to inform students about exactly where to obtain information is bound to be largely out of date and irrelevant before it is published. Still, by learning the underlying theories and general methods of investigative research, an investigator will be much better poised to adapt to this fluid environment. In any case, having persistence and the ability to adapt quickly will take an investigator a very long way toward obtaining the information she is looking for.

Information is generally categorized as either **government data** or **private-sector data**. In the former category, many government agencies routinely compile information about people and businesses, and much of this information is available to investigators who know where to look. For example, courts maintain records about all types of criminal and civil litigation; various regulatory agencies maintain records regarding applicable registrations and enforcement actions; motor vehicle administrations maintain records regarding licensed drivers and their vehicles;

state boards of elections keep records about registered voters; and law enforcement agencies store records regarding arrests and investigations. It is best to think of government records relevant to investigations first as either state or federal records, and then as either records arising from the executive or judicial branches of the applicable government. An investigator is typically only concerned with records stored by the legislative branch insofar as those records are ratified into laws.

At both the state and federal level, many records of the executive branches of government are now available online simply by visiting the agency's website and searching for a link to the agency's database. For example, an investigator searching for the whereabouts of a federal prisoner need only visit the Federal Bureau of Prisons to search their handy inmate locater, and an investigator searching for information about a doctor's credentials in Virginia may go to the website for the Virginia Department of Professional and Occupational Regulation. Some government databases only grant access to private investigators and other individuals who qualify to open an account with the agency. For example, many state departments of motor vehicles grant access to private investigative businesses, but not to the general public.[2]

Those records that are not available online but are otherwise public records are often available via the Freedom of Information Act (FOIA). Both federal and state FOIA requests are made by preparing a formal letter and delivering it to the applicable executive agency. Note that following the U.S. Supreme Court's decision in *McBurney v. Young*,[3] access to some state records could be denied to private investigators who are not residents of those states where the records are maintained, meaning that in some instances it may be necessary to hire a local investigator to file an out-of-state FOIA request.

What constitutes a public record is sometimes a matter of interpretation by the agency that houses the record. Any record concerning an ongoing investigation, telephone and banking records, airline passenger manifests, and any document deemed sensitive to national security is probably not public. Likewise, records that contain private information about individual citizens are also not public, unless the subject provides a signed release of information. This does not, however, apply to state voter and tax registrations and to property records. Sometimes even if a portion of a document is deemed private, the agency will simply redact the private parts with a black marker or its digital equivalent, and then release the document. In any case, an investigator should never assume that just because she could not locate a particular type of record on a government agency's website, that the record is not public. Likewise, she should not assume that having an FOIA request rejected constitutes the final word on whether the desired record is public or not. Often FOIA requests are summarily denied the first time and must be appealed for reconsideration, and persistence pays off.

The federal and state judicial branches of government are the most prolific keepers of public records in the public sector. Because access to law enforcement criminal record repositories is extremely limited for investigators in the private sector, typically requiring the release of the subject, most criminal record searches by private investigators are conducted using **court records**. Courts also maintain records related to bankruptcies, probate matters, divorces, and other civil cases, providing a plethora of potential sources of information for investigators. Almost all court cases are public records, save matters related to children (e.g., juvenile criminal proceedings), which are generally sealed by the court. Some states also restrict access to marriage and divorce records. Sometimes these records will not be released without a court order.

During the past decade, public court records have become increasingly available online, making court research far easier for investigators than it used to be. Federal court records, including bankruptcies, are now available online via the Public Access to Court Electronic Records (PACER) system, and many state court records are now available online, as well. However, some jurisdictions are still not available online and must be searched in person or via telephone. In the event that online records do not exist in a particular jurisdiction, the investigator should call the clerk of that court and ask about the procedures for searching and obtaining copies of records. Unfortunately, this sometimes involves prepaying for the records with a check, a process that can take several weeks. When the investigator needs the records sooner, she may instead hire a local investigator, preferably identified through a shared investigative association, to conduct the search for her. As an alternative to hiring a contract investigator, some database firms also offer onsite searches for a nominal fee. They are able to charge so little because they operate in bulk searches for multiple clients. For example, a database firm may send their own contract investigator to a particular courthouse to conduct upwards of fifty searches per day for clients all over the country. An investigator using these services can typically expect a 24- to 48-hour turnaround before receiving the results of her search.

In terms of records maintained by the private sector (e.g., payroll records, phone records, etc.), a lot of information useful to investigators is available by simply searching the web. Information not available on the web can be obtained from private companies with a subpoena *duces tecum*, or by simply asking or bartering for it. When searching for records online, a distinction must be made between the **Internet** and the **web**.[4] The Internet is a set of rules that allow computers to communicate and connect with other computers, while the web is a graphic software interface that allows computer users to more easily obtain and disseminate information to other computers throughout the world. These distinctions are important because they highlight the limitations of conducting a so-called search on the web, which is only a portion of what might otherwise be available for those who know where to look. Also, they highlight the fact that *where* to look for information online and *how* to garner access depends wholly on who you are and what type of information you are looking for. It is easiest to think of the web as the public part of the Internet, keeping in mind that even large parts of the web are not easily available for those not granted access. Some online activities conducted using the Internet, such as checking email and sharing files with other computer users, can be conducted outside the purview of the web and are entirely private endeavors. There is, therefore, no way for investigators to legally access this information without a subpoena. Moreover, since the web is not a "thing," per se, as much as a conglomeration of millions of separate computers, even access to information on the web is determined solely by the keeper of the particular data. While some entities help establish policy for how the web operates—and certain companies (e.g., Microsoft) have influence over the evolution of its infrastructure—nobody actually controls the web or access to the data therein, except insofar as federal and state governments prohibit unlawful theft of information, sometimes referred to as hacking.

Keeping the above in mind, running a query in a search engine is not synonymous to conducting a search of the web, and much less so of the entire Internet. A search engine is merely a database of public websites collected by software robots (described below). Each search engine uses widely disparate variables that weigh the relevance of those sites to the terms that an investigator searched, and they provide those websites to her in a list, typically with a synopsis of the content of each website. In many instances, the websites of companies that paid for advertising are ranked higher in the search results. Because each search engine is completely different than the others, no two searches on different search engines will yield the exact same result. All search engines have three components: the robot, the indexer, and the query process.[5] The robot is similar to a web browser (e.g., Mozilla's Firefox), seeking out websites, copying them completely, and then following links to other websites, indefinitely—although a robot is automated and much faster than a browser. The robot then sends the copied websites that it has identified to the indexer, which employs mathematical algorithms to categorize and classify the data from the websites. Only after these two steps have been completed does the data become available to the queries of users of the web. The query process is a function of each individual search engine determining the relevance of its millions of stored websites using complicated and proprietary algorithms, to the search terms used in the query.

This is all to say that, although useful as a starting point for investigations, data obtained from web search engines is based only upon a highly filtered and, in many cases, arbitrary interpretation of what is relevant to an investigator, depending on the search terms she put into the search engine during the query process. Search engines are therefore more useful for investigators to obtain general biographical data about people and companies for later use when conducting other methods of investigative research. For example, if an investigator only knows a witness she is trying to find by the name of John Smith, but she also knows that he was once a broker at the now-defunct Bear Stearns securities brokerage firm, she might, by searching the terms "John * Smith" (where the asterisk represents a wildcard) coupled with "Bear Sterns," learn that the subject's full name is John Edward Smith. In this example, the subject's middle name is an example of a **non-biometric identifier**, which is anything that helps an investigator differentiate one person named John Smith from all of the other thousands of people in the United States with the same forename and surname. Non-biometric identifiers also include Social Security numbers, dates of birth, prior addresses, and any other information that may help differentiate one person from another. A biometric identifier, on the other hand, is something that is biological, such as a fingerprint or DNA.

Beyond the basic web searches conducted by investigators using browsers, there is a great deal of information available on the web that is beyond the surface of these cursory searches. This content explicitly includes social media, such as Facebook, Twitter, blogs, wikis, chat rooms, and discussion forums. The distinctions between the different types of social media are not vitally important for our purposes; they all represent methods of disseminating information online, primarily user-generated content. From an investigative standpoint, social media websites like Facebook, for example, are distinguishable from other web content because the information contained on Facebook is often only viewable by people who have subscribed to the webpage and who have been afforded access according to the privacy settings of the company that controls the data and, in many cases, the users themselves. In essence, the information is stored in a password protected venue where robots cannot index the information and make it available to search engines. Therefore, much of the information in social media and other pseudo-private venues will not appear in common web searches.

Investigators who know where to look, however, can subscribe to social media websites, even using an undercover identity (under certain limitations, described below) to obtain information without concern of violating anyone's reasonable expectation of privacy. Social media and dating websites, for example, which both have a chat and a pseudo-blog component, typically require an account to glean access, and sometimes the consent of the subject, such as through a "friend" request (e.g., on Facebook). An investigator may access this information by joining these websites, setting up a profile, and soliciting the subject's consent, if necessary, thereby gaining access to the subject's publicly posted information. Keep in mind, however, there may be ethical and legal considerations in some instances with assuming an undercover identity. An investigator should never assume the identity of a person who actually exists, which could constitute criminal identity theft in some jurisdictions. Furthermore, it is unethical to contact witnesses for the purpose of interviewing them without properly identifying yourself, and this is equally true when contacting witnesses using social media websites.[6]

Aside from the information available on the web, there are plenty of companies that sell data for a fee to licensed private investigators and others. These companies are often termed "databases" in the popular investigative vernacular; despite that many of them are not technically databases at all. These companies form contractual relationships with credit reporting agencies, courts, law enforcement agencies and the like, and then make their information available to investigators. The information offered by these companies may help an investigator locate people; find unlisted telephone numbers; identify the owners and values of real property and vehicles; find information regarding liens and judgments; and locate a myriad of other public data. Although some of the information available from these databases for a fee is actually public in other places (e.g., court records), they do all of the work for the investigator. Plus, some of the information, such as unlisted telephone numbers, is *not* otherwise publicly available. Popular databases include CLEAR, Tracers Information, TLO, and Accurint. Which databases to use is largely determined by the investigator's preference. Because some databases have recently begun truncating or redacting the last four digits of subjects' Social Security numbers from search results out of a concern for privacy (e.g., 123-45-****), private investigators have increasingly relied on the databases that do not truncate their data. Not having a full Social Security number limits the non-biometric data available to an investigator for subsequent research.

Information that is not available online, via a FOIA request or through a database, may still be public. Private companies that maintain records have the exclusive authority to release that information to a third party, provided its release conforms to their policies and applicable privacy laws—and provided it suits their interests. The bottom line is that it never hurts to ask a company to release information voluntarily, pointing out how cooperating may benefit them or even society in some way. For example, property managers will routinely provide information to private investigators without a subpoena, often because they like having information about their tenants. Even telephone companies may voluntarily release call records if they believe they have a vested interest in the outcome of the investigation, such as in an investigation intended to catch people defrauding consumers using their telephone or Internet services.

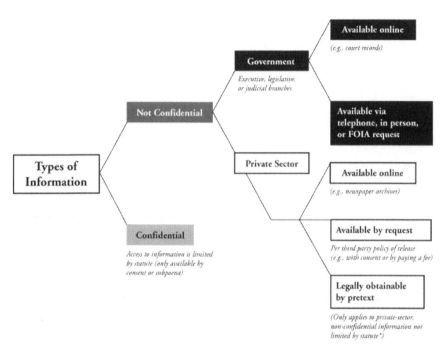

Federal law expressly bans the pretexting of financial, health, and confidential telephone records.

Practical Exercise: *Conduct research on yourself or someone you know, searching for as much information as possible. Use at least two sources of government data, only one of which may be court records, and two sources of private sector data, only one of which may be from the Internet. What government sources did you use, and how did you access this data? What private-sector sources did you use, and what means did you use to access this information?*

5

Interviewing

After the prisoner abuse scandal at Abu Ghraib in Iraq and the subsequent national debate about torture, there is much confusion about the difference between investigative **interviewing** and **interrogation**. Interrogation has become something of a dirty word in the national lexicon, although there is nothing inherently improper about the conduction of an interrogation by an investigator. Conducting interrogations is a special skill that requires intense training and practice, and this section will therefore focus exclusively on the more general and versatile skill of conducting interviews. However, it is essential first to differentiate between the two skill sets, which are both methods of verbally obtaining information from subjects, so as to be clear about what an interview is and *is not* vis-à-vis the semantically unpopular (and arguably misunderstood) practice of interrogation. Most significantly, an interview is a non-accusatory dialogue, where the primary purpose is to illicit information about the facts in question during an investigation.[7] A dialogue is a back-and-forth conversation with questions followed by responses or answers. Both investigator and subject are active participants in the process: question, pause, response, recording of response, next question, etc. An interrogation, on the other hand, is an accusatory monologue, and, in contrast, the primary purpose is to illicit a confession of guilt from a subject. Also, because of the back-and-forth nature of an interview, it is customary and preferred, although not necessarily required, that an investigator take notes during an interview, whereas an investigator never takes notes during an interrogation until after the subject has confessed. The primary reason is that, during an interrogation, the presence of a pen and notepad remind the subject of the fact that, should he confess, his words will later be used against him. Another major difference between interviews and interrogations is that interviews tend to be shorter and can even be structured, if necessary, to fit within a given timeframe. For example, if the subject is on a lunch break and only has thirty minutes of free time, the investigator could conduct the interview within that window of time. In contrast, one of the goals of an interrogation is to create the impression of unlimited time. If the investigator attempts to conduct an interrogation within a specifically defined timeframe, many subjects will simply run out the clock, so to speak.

Another important distinction is that between an **investigative interview** and a **polygraph examination**. Similar to an investigative interview, a polygraph exam involves questions posed by the examiner and then a careful analysis of the subject's responses. During an interview, the investigator must evaluate the subject's behavioral responses, keeping in mind that behavior may be verbal, nonverbal, or paralinguistic (discussed below). Unlike an interview, however, a polygraph exam evaluates certain physiological symptoms of a subject, particularly his heart rate, blood pressure, respiratory rate, and electro-dermal activity, in response to closed questions. The theory behind both investigative interviews and polygraph exams is that a subject experiences anxiety during deception that manifests itself in physical symptoms that are observable by the investigator or by the polygraph machine. Blind studies have shown there is a correlation, albeit a weak one, between lying subjects and subjects flagged as deceptive during polygraph exams, and similar patterns have been documented during studies of behavioral analysis interviews. Where the two methods diverge, however, is that proponents of polygraph exams purport that their methods are scientific, whereas proponents of behavioral analysis claim only that an investigative interview is a useful technique for obtaining more accurate information during an investigation. Where a polygraph exam is most useful is in the underlying belief in subjects that the exam is highly accurate and capable of picking up deception. After being confronted with the results of a failed polygraph exam, subjects often make a full confession.

However, with the benefit that the guise of science affords to polygraph exams comes the high cost of heavy state and federal regulation. For example, in Virginia, all polygraph examiners must be licensed and all exams require the written consent of the examinee.[8] There are also strict rules regarding the prior notification of examinees, the duration and frequency of sessions, record keeping and the like. Also, no questions may be asked regarding the subject's lawful political or religious activities, or about his sexual preferences. The licensing procedures for examiners in Virginia require that the applicant have either five years' investigative experience relevant to conducting polygraphs, completion of a state-approved polygraph training school, and a six-month apprenticeship. However, the two-year training requirement may be satisfied with an associate's degree, and all five years may be satisfied with a bachelor's degree. All applicants must also pass an exam and undergo a background check. On the federal level, the Employee Polygraph Protection Act of 1988 (EPPA) almost universally prohibits polygraph examinations in the private sector, unless used in an investigation involving economic loss, where reasonable suspicion exists that the subject was involved in the crime.[9] Unlike with an investigative interview, employees may *not* be terminated for refusing to submit to a polygraph exam. They may not even be terminated solely on the basis of the results of the polygraph exam. Obviously, because of these restrictions, polygraphs are of very limited use in most private-sector investigations. They are more often employed in government background investigations and in private-sector background investigations where there are specific exemptions carved out by the EPPA, such as in the security and pharmaceutical industries.

> **Discussion:** *Name at least three differences between an interview and an interrogation. What are three disadvantages of conducting a polygraph exam as opposed to an investigative interview? What are the advantages of conducting a polygraph exam?*

Conducting an Investigative Interview

A far more versatile tool for gathering information is the investigative interview. Before an interview can begin, the investigator must first establish **rapport** with the subject. This is typically accomplished within the first few minutes of the interview. During social (i.e., non-investigative) interviews, rapport is often accomplished using the practice of elicitation, which is an indirect way of obtaining information by asking only indirect questions. Using elicitation, parents, for example, often deduct that their teenager wrecked the car, not by asking them directly if they got into an accident, but by asking them how they are doing and carefully, but surreptitiously, gauging their behavior during the response.

Rapport is defined as a relationship of trust, or the degree to which a subject is comfortable during an interview. Rapport serves to decrease the subject's internal tension and allows the investigator to establish the subject's normal pattern of behavior, sometimes referred to as norming or calibrating a subject. By recognizing a subject's normal pattern of behavior, an investigator can infer meaning from behaviors that deviate from that norm later in the interview. Although the notion of trust is highly subjective, it is possible for an investigator to increase or decrease the degree of rapport during an interview. One way to establish rapport is through casual, non-threatening conversation about such topics as the weather, sports, or the like. This is akin to the natural process of elicitation. It is not advisable, however, to become too friendly with a subject. The investigator wants the subject to feel comfortable, but she must also retain control of the interview and firmly lead the questioning. Investigators overly concerned with rapport beyond the first few minutes risk giving the subject tacit permission to lie during the interview. In many ways, rapport is the antithesis of tension. Imagine a novice investigator who harshly barks questions at an unwitting subject. In such a tense interview, there would be a near complete absence of rapport. On the other side of the spectrum, imagine another novice investigator spending an inordinate amount of time engaged in elicitation, establishing rapport with a subject—waxing about politics and the other unrelated topics—but decidedly avoiding questions related to the issue under investigation in a misguided effort to keep the subject feeling comfortable. This interview would have a near complete absence of tension. Both novice investigators are unlikely to glean much information from the subject, the first because she failed to establish enough rapport, and the second because she allowed herself to become too concerned about rapport, to the detriment of any substantive questioning.

A good way to illustrate the dynamics of an interview is by considering the hypothetically perfect interview: a single open question followed by a subject responding truthfully, in a single response, with all the details pertinent to the issue under investigation. In the perfect interview, the investigator need not concern herself with follow-up questions or whether the subject is lying or withholding information; all of the material information came out in response to the very first question. Obviously, this scenario posits an unrealistic ideal, one highly unlikely to occur during a real interview. Although there are several reasons why this hypothetical interview almost never occurs in reality, a couple of the most significant factors include: the need for the investigator to fully inform the subject about the scope of the issue under investigation, and the inhibition of the disclosure of information caused by the subject's internal anxiety. While the former issue can be rectified to some degree by a clear introduction and skilled question formation, including appropriate follow-up questions, the latter issue requires the investigator to establish rapport with the subject to relieve internal anxiety that may inhibit information.

A subject's internal anxiety may be caused by anger, shame, fear, or any number of other emotions related or unrelated to the issue under investigation. A subject may be fearful of being caught during deception, or may be embarrassed for a completely unrelated reason. In either case, the subject's internal anxiety is likely to inhibit his communication during an interview. The investigator can increase rapport by maintaining a non-judgmental attitude and expressing sincere interest in the subject's responses. But beyond these basics, the key to establishing rapport is identifying the possible causes of the subject's internal anxiety and *indirectly* addressing those factors that are possibly inhibiting communication. It is not necessary or prudent to directly address or attempt to negotiate the possible causes of a subject's anxiety, because this may backfire and serve to actually *decrease* rapport. People are generally socialized to believe that emotionally stimulating or controversial topics should be avoided with strangers. For example, if a subject seems hesitant to provide information, and it seems likely that he may be ashamed to admit that he lied in a previous statement to another investigator, the investigator may increase rapport by not avowing knowledge of the subject's previous statement. The problem with this approach, however, is that a deceptive subject will perceive the interviewer's unwillingness to confront his deception as tacit approval to lie without anxiety. It is therefore necessary to strike a balance between rapport and tension during an interview by being friendly—but not too friendly—with the subject.

Once the investigator has established a degree of rapport with the subject, the next consideration is the interview **location** and **setting**. The hypothetically perfect interview setting is conducted within a small room with no windows or artwork, containing two chairs spaced approximately four to six feet apart, with no barriers between them. The suspect sits in one chair and the investigator in the other. The sparsely decorated room allows for freedom from distractions and barriers that might inhibit communication. While such an environment may not be practical in every situation, an approximation of these principles should guide an investigator's consideration of a setting. In interviews conducted offsite, the investigator should attempt to steer the subject to a setting that most approximates this ideal. Kitchens work well in residential locations, and interviewing a subject inside a vehicle is a prudent method if the interview must be conducted out on the street. Both alternatives afford the greatest amount of control over these environments.

The hypothetically perfect interview setting is two chairs, approximately four to six feet apart, positioned so they are directly facing each other. There should be no barriers between the investigator and the subject, and as few distractions as possible. Distractions can inhibit communication and make it more difficult for the investigator to interpret the subject's behavior.

While practically the opposite of the perfect interview setting, telephone interviews are sometimes necessary because of budgetary constraints or distance. These interviews can still be effective, although there are several disadvantages that must be considered. For example, social factors, namely the scourge of telemarketers who have made it socially acceptable to hang up on strangers, tend to make subjects statistically less likely to cooperate during an interview over the telephone. Additionally, telephone interviews limit investigators to hearing only a subject's verbal and paralinguistic responses (discussed below). This makes in-person interviews preferable over telephone interviews. In instances where it is necessary to conduct an interview by telephone, the investigator should be prepared to spend more time establishing rapport. Such interviews also require repeated attempts to garner cooperation, as subjects are apt to screen telephone calls. For interviews with cooperative subjects, my firm has had a great deal of success conducting interviews via video conference services, such as Skype.

During in-person interviews, from a purely investigative standpoint, it is always better to conduct an interview one-on-one: investigator and subject. This environment allows for the greatest amount of rapport and the fewest distractions. Sometimes, however, such an interview may not be possible, or it might be prudent to have a witness present. With the exception of a union representative or an attorney—and both only in rare cases—there are few legal requirements for having a third party present during an interview. There are several practical instances, however, when having a third party present is practical for an investigator, such as when an interpreter is needed, or during an interview when it is believed that a subject may later accuse the investigator of acting improperly. If the concerns are of a sexual nature, the investigator should choose a witness who is the same gender as the subject. Whenever a third party attends an interview, the investigator should instruct the extra party to sit outside the subject's line of sight, with one notable exception: interpreters should be instructed to sit immediately adjacent to the investigator, both facing the subject. This is because subjects invariably turn to look at interpreters when they are speaking, which is harmful to the rapport between investigator and subject.

The length of an interview is largely affected by the nature of the issue under investigation. Most interviews should last about thirty minutes to one hour, but complicated issues may require several hours of interview time, sometimes involving several interviews dispersed throughout several days. There are diminishing returns when attempting to conduct a complicated interview that takes several hours in one setting, but there is no firm rule with regard to the maximum time that an interview should last. With interviews that last over three hours, rapport can diminish and the subject may get restless and irritable. If further interviewing is required after several hours, the investigator should consider scheduling the remainder of the interview for the following day, if feasible. Otherwise, the time of the interview is largely dictated by the subject matter and the subject's schedule.

During interviews conducted at the investigator's office or a similar location where a subject is unfamiliar, outright refusal to grant break requests, or not allowing a subject to voluntarily stop an interview in the private-sector is likely to bring about an allegation of duress and may even be tantamount to false imprisonment. **Duress** is not a legal action; rather it is a defense, typically by a criminal defendant, who argues that an admission should be inadmissible in court. This defense generally occurs when a subject only confessed because he found the interview environment intolerable and was not free to leave. Although many subjects claim they were under duress when they offered a confession, the easiest test for whether duress actually occurred is by evaluating whether the subject made any attempts to leave the interview and was prevented from doing so.[10] It is generally okay to *gently* dissuade a subject from taking an immediate break, when the investigator believes that a break will stifle an impending and significant breakthrough because of the inevitable loss of momentum. However, save when the breakthrough is deemed to be highly significant to the outcome of the case, it is always better to grant and even offer frequent breaks, to supply non-alcoholic drinks and food, and to otherwise make the subject feel as comfortable as possible, while continuing to strike the proper balance between rapport and tension. If a subject unequivocally requests to stop the interview, it is imperative that the investigator allow him to do so. However, the investigator should listen very carefully to what the subject says in this regard, because even such phrases as, "I really do not want to be involved in this anymore," do not necessarily constitute a concrete decision to stop. The investigator is permitted to attempt to persuade a subject to continue participating with an interview, provided she does not stand in his way of exiting or otherwise make it appear to a "reasonable person" that he is not free to leave the interview at any time.

The principles of **basic questioning** dictate that individual questions should be limited to one topic at a time and not be leading or negative.

A negative question is a type of closed, leading question where the investigator leads the subject to a negative assumption. An example of a negative question is, "You didn't steal the money, did you?" Leading questions are problematic because they are pre-qualified and are therefore very easy to lie to. The proper question in this example is, "Did you steal the money?" An investigator should start with innocuous questions designed to establish a subject's normal pattern of behavior in response to questions, and should then flow to open, open/clarifying questions, and finally to closed questions, in that order. In the perfect interview, the investigator needs only to ask one question to obtain all the information she needs, for example: "What happened?" This is an open question, because it can be answered in an infinite number of ways. Because the subject has many response options to an open question, he tends to experience less internal anxiety than with a more limiting question type. The key to interpreting responses to open questions is listening very carefully to the response and speculating what the subject may be leaving out. All interviews should begin with open questions, because these questions, by causing little anxiety, help to establish rapport and also provide the most content-laden responses, which can be employed to good use later in the interview process. After open questions come open/clarifying questions, which are follow-up questions that elicit more detail from a portion of an open response that was lacking in clarity. An example of an open/clarifying question is:

You told me a minute ago that you left work yesterday around 2 p.m., and that you got home sometime in the afternoon. What did you do between the time you left work and when you got home?

The open/clarifying question is open, insofar as it allows the subject to relay the information in response to the question in a nearly infinite number of ways, but, because the question imposes some constraints on the possible scope of the response, it is more focused than a purely open question.

Finally, closed questions provide for only a one-word or otherwise short response, typically "yes" or "no." They are highly limited in scope and tend to produce greater amounts of tension during the interview. In the above example, a possible closed question might be, "Did you arrive home after 3 p.m.?" Because closed questions create more anxiety, they have the benefit of producing more interpretable nonverbal and paralinguistic behavior. In contrast, open and open/clarifying questions elicit more verbal information, but not much meaningful nonverbal and paralinguistic behavior.

Outside of basic questioning skills, there are many techniques to elicit more information from a reluctant, uncooperative, or untruthful witness. These are termed **admission seeking questions**. Although an interrogation is oftentimes the only way to elicit an actual admission of guilt from a suspect, sometimes an interrogation is impractical given the circumstances. When a subject qualifies his language regarding whether an event occurred or not, often a hypothetical question can be an effective follow up, especially if an affirmation of the *possibility* of something happening is tantamount to an admission that it happened. An example of a hypothetical question might be, in response to a subject's claim that he cannot remember if his friend told him about the whereabouts of stolen money, "Is it possible that he told you where the money is, and you just forgot?" In this example, if the subject admits that it is possible his friend told him about the money, then he cannot later credibly claim that the conversation did *not* occur. In other words, when a subject uses a lack of memory as a means of evading a topic, an investigator can use a hypothetical question to fill in the blanks of what could have happened, thereby having fodder to impeach a witness's testimony should he later claim that it decidedly did not happen.

Another useful admission seeking tactic is the **alternative question**. In the context of an interrogation, an alternative question is when the investigator poses two possible scenarios to a subject and asks him which one is correct, where both responses are essentially admissions to the underlying event, but one paints the subject in a more unfavorable light than the other. In an interrogation, for example, the investigator might ask, "We already know you stole the money, but did you just intend to 'borrow' it so that you could feed your starving family—or did you steal it to buy drugs?" While alternative questions posed during interrogations are outside the scope of this book, a more general type of alternative question can be used effectively during an interview. For example, when interviewing a subject who initially claims not to have witnessed an event under investigation, asking him the following can be quite effective:

Look, about ten people told me they saw you there—but what I really need to know is whether you were there from the beginning or whether you just came by when the car pulled up.

In this example, even if the subject only admits to witnessing half the event, the investigator has still circumvented his initial denial of knowledge.

Another type of admission seeking question is a **bait question**, which is a type of hypothetical question. A bait question occurs when a subject, who has already provided a detailed account, is presented with the possibility of conflicting evidence and is asked if it is possible that he was mistaken in his earlier statement. The hypothetical evidence presented during a bait question is often not real; the investigator sometimes just makes it up. For example, a subject who has adamantly maintained that he never saw a particular document could be asked if there is any reason why his fingerprints might be found on it. In this example, the investigator might not know whether the subject's fingerprints were found on the document or not, and she may not even have an intention of testing the document for fingerprints. The deception is legally and ethically permissible because it would not persuade an innocent person to confess to something he did not do. The subject who did not, in fact, touch the document, will respond to this bait question with an unequivocal and firm denial. On the other hand, if the subject exhibits behavior that appears deceptive or backpedals significantly from his earlier story, he probably handled the document. Bait questions are primarily useful for identifying deception, but not to achieve an actual confession. It is therefore imperative that an investigator always allow the subject a way to "save face" during a bait question, i.e., to explain away the inconsistency without admitting deception. Also, most reasonably intelligent subjects typically catch on after the second time a bait question is employed by an investigator during an interview, causing her to then lose credibility in the subject's eyes. It is therefore better to use a maximum of one bait question per interview.

The final means of eliciting admissions during an investigative interviews involves directly confronting a subject about his inconsistencies or conflicting evidence, although this should only be used as a last resort. This tactic can be a catalyst for confrontation, where the subject decidedly stops the interview. It also tips the investigator's hand about what she knows about the case, information that might, for example, be better saved for trial. However, in some cases, confronting a subject about inconsistencies can be a powerful way to ramp up tension during an interview and amplify the subject's behavioral symptoms to determine which version is the lie and which is the truth. This tactic works best when the evidence is strong and irrefutable, and when it directly contradicts information the subject previously told the investigator during the interview.

Notwithstanding the aforementioned questioning techniques, the most important part of conducting an interview is the art of **listening** and **observing**. Note taking is preferable during an interview, in part because it slows down the pace of the interview, thereby allowing the investigator to more carefully listen to the subject's responses and to observe his behavior. Words are the building blocks of speech, but it is important to realize they are only symbols. Which symbols a subject uses to depict objects or events is a matter of personal choice. Although lies can be manifested in nonverbal behavior, lying only occurs at the verbal level through the choice of words that a subject uses. Further-more, the choice of words has a different meaning in different contexts of the interview. A verbal narrative describes either a subject's subjec-tive interpretation of himself in relation to an event and other parties associated with that event—or it describes what the subject *wants* the interviewer to believe about those same relationships. Because decep-tion and confrontation creates internal anxiety for a subject, word choices often attempt to alleviate that anxiety by avoiding overt decep-tion or outright confrontation. Therefore, a subject rarely *chooses* to lie to or confront the investigator, and will generally not do so unless he perceives no other response options. Carefully listening to the words that a subject chooses can provide valuable information about what he will *not* tell you directly about the "objective" truth of the event in ques-tion. It is important to remember that words are deliberate symbols and must be considered in their verbatim form. Basing an assumption on what a subject *probably* meant is a grave error during an interview.

In response to each question posed by an investigator, a subject may exercise four possible response categories: telling the truth; omitting all or part of the truth; evading the truth by verbal implication; or outright lying. It is important to understand that, because there are so many possible response options to open questions, subjects rarely lie outright to these questions; they are far more likely to tell the truth, engage in omission, and then engage in evasion, in that order. Verbally truthful responses tend to directly and unequivocally answer the question that was asked. In other words, they will make logical sense and will not em-ploy unrealistic qualifiers. A **qualifier** is anything that lessens a subject's commitment to his response. For example, a subject who states, "The gunman was wearing a black mask," is much more likely to be telling the truth than someone who claims:

I think the gunman was wearing a black mask. I do not really remember. It was two weeks ago.

Qualifiers usually imply uncertainty with regard to memory or belief. In evaluating whether a qualifier is unreasonable, the investigator should put herself in the subject's position and ask herself what she would likely believe or remember under those same circumstances. For example, it may be reasonable for a subject to employ a memory qualifier for something that happened two months ago, but not for something that happened yesterday. Likewise, people who experience a traumatic event tend to have a heightened state of memory related to the circumstances of that event. An investigator should therefore expect a subject to remember such an event and should suspect deception if he does not.

A truthful subject will volunteer information without being asked and, if accused of a crime, employ realistic language about the crime in his denial. Truthful responses to open questions also tend to be much longer on average than untruthful responses. This is because a truthful subject has nothing to hide and typically wants to help the investigation. For criminal cases, truthful subjects are more likely to refer to the crime under investigation using realistic and adequately descriptive language. In other words, it would be more indicative of a truthful response to declare, "I did not rape that woman!" than to state, "I did not have anything to do with that thing she's accusing me of." In these examples, a subject who uses the term "rape" is psychologically comfortable calling the alleged crime what it is, whereas the subject who refers to it by the vague description, "that thing," is clearly experiencing a higher degree of anxiety, which could be indicative of deception. A truthful subject will also typically use explanatory terms showing cause and effect, such as "since" and "because." This verbal behavior demonstrates a reasoned and reasonable way of recalling and describing information, relevant to the issue under investigation.

The next verbal response category is **omission**, which is simply editing or withholding information. An investigator should be most attuned to omission when evaluating verbal responses to open questions, because this is when it most often occurs. Of the deceptive response options, omission causes the least internal stress. Signs of omission include talking off topic, withholding relevant information, *temporal lacunae* (discussed below), repression, and a lack of appropriate detail. Investigators will typically recognize a response that has details omitted because it does not make factual sense; there is some piece to the story that is apparently missing to make it complete. Possible signs that something is missing are **temporal lacunae**, which are lapses in part of the narrative, usually preceding terms such as "then," "later on," or "after that"—when the terms do not actually follow the logical sequence they imply. For example, imagine the following narrative given by a person accused of committing an assault, where the victim had to receive emergency medical treatment:

Well, we got into a tussle, and then he punched me in the head. I was just trying to defend myself. And then I was running down the street, and all of these dudes were chasing me.

The lack of content between the word "myself" and the sentence where he describes running down the street is a *temporal lacuna*, because it leaves out a significant part of the narrative; the point when the alleged assault on the victim occurred. Also in the above example, the word "tussle" is an example of both unrealistic language and an inappropriate lack of detail. The investigator must ask herself if the term "tussle" adequately describes an event that caused someone to go to the emergency room. If not, then something is missing, and the subject is omitting some critical piece of information. This is not to say that the subject in the above account is necessarily lying, but the investigator certainly must delve into the narrative in more detail with additional questions to determine what facts are being omitted and why. Another tactic of omission is **repression**, which is an unrealistic lack of memory recall, such as when a subject claims he cannot remember the basic details of a traumatic or memorable event that occurred within a short temporal proximity to the interview. Keep in mind that most events worth investigating were traumatic in some way for the people involved. An investigator should be skeptical of subjects who claim not to remember an event that most reasonable people would clearly have remembered.

After omission, the next category of responses is **evasion**, most commonly seen in responses to open/clarifying and closed questions, where subjects find that omission is no longer an effective method of deception. Evasion walks a fine line between omission and outright deception. When subjects evade, they lie by implication. The telltale signs of evasive responses include unrealistic language and qualifiers, negation, specific denials, and weakened assertions. We have already discussed qualifiers above. **Negation** occurs when a subject describes what did *not* happen, rather than what actually happened. For example, assume that a manager is the subject of a harassment investigation. He is asked what he did during a particular lunch break, and he replies:

> *I never even laid my hands on her. I don't know what the hell she is talking about! I deny this incident categorically!*

In this example, the subject is engaged in negation, because he is only telling the investigator what did *not* happen. Assuming the underlying allegation involved the manager using one of his hands to inappropriately touch his co-worker, it would also be an example of a specific denial. Technically speaking, he did not lay his "hands" on the woman; he only laid *one* hand on her. His use of the term "incident" is also indicative of unrealistic language, used to psychologically distance a subject from something that he is too afraid or ashamed to say out loud during the interview.

Another tool of the evasive is a **weakened assertion**, which is when a subject implies that he began to engage in some activity, but it is unclear from his response whether the action was actually completed. By using phrases like, "I started to," "I needed to," and "I began to," a subject is sometimes able to trick novice investigators into improperly inferring that the action was completed, when it actually was not. Consider the following narrative:

> *The first thing I always do before I make the deposit is to count the checks, which I then tally up, and then I put the totals on a spreadsheet. On this day, I started to add up the checks, which is around the time that I got a call from Brian, who talked my ear off for about ten minutes. When I finally was able to put all the figures from the checks I counted onto the spreadsheet, it was almost 6 p.m. I didn't even make it to the bank until 6:10 p.m., when it was already closed. So I took the checks home and made the deposit the next morning.*

In this example, the subject never states that he completed counting all the checks—only that he added up the checks that he counted. Notice that he begins by discussing how he normally processed the deposits, not how he processed them on this day. This is a classic example of a weakened assertion. Catching these types of evasive responses requires incredible attention to detail on the part of the investigator.

Subjects who find their attempts to omit or evade unsuccessful will ultimately choose to either lie or tell the truth. Blatant deception typically occurs in response to closed questions, because this is when a subject has no other response options—assuming a skilled investigator will not allow him to evade these questions. When deception occurs in response to open or open/clarifying questions, it is typically indicative of a rehearsed account. In these instances, subjects will rattle off their rehearsed narrative to the first open question like a laundry list, sometimes even accentuating each element with a number or a letter. Investigators call this deceptive behavior "listing." Verbal signs of deception include responses repeating simply-worded questions, statements against self-interest, unnecessary bolstering, and overly polite or "phony" behavior. One of the most telltale signs of deception is actually a paralinguistic trait—**response latency**—which is the delay between when a question ends and the start of the subject's response. Subjects sometimes attempt to verbally mask response latency by repeating simply worded questions or employing stalling mechanisms, such as "let's see," "well," and "um." Whether a latent response is indicative of deception or not depends to a large extent on the question. Responses to questions that call for memory recall or speculation are normally significantly latent in any account, truthful or not, because it takes the subject time to formulate a response. This intuitively makes sense, because lying is fundamentally the act of invention, and speculation is also a mentally inventive task. While memory is not inventive, per se, occurring in a different portion of the brain, it is similarly time consuming. Straight-forward questions, however, should not be significantly latent, and subjects who parrot these questions or use stalling methods are delaying their responses for some other reason, possibly to concoct a lie.

Other indicators of deception include such expressions as, "I swear to god" and "I swear on my mother's grave." These expressions are termed unnecessary bolstering because deceptive subjects are attempting to bolster their credibility with these meaningless platitudes. They are highly indicative of deception. Similarly, statements against self-interest are also highly correlated with deception. A statement against self-interest is when a subject starts a response with a phrase such as, "You're probably not going to believe this, but...," or "I know this sounds like a crazy story, but..." Deceptive subjects use these hackneyed phrases because they are experiencing a high degree of anxiety and feel compelled to buttress their story with phases they believe will make them sound more truthful. Closely related to these behaviors is overly polite, inappropriately flirtatious, or outright phony behavior. Flattery and brown-nosing are often ploys to attempt to disarm an investigator. When a subject tells an investigator, for example, that she has a very interesting job, has pretty eyes and the like, this is often an attempt by a subject to divert attention from himself. Whenever a subject engages in this type of behavior, an investigator should suspect that the subject has something to hide.

Although lying only occurs at the verbal level, it is also possible to detect deception from the nonverbal behavior and paralinguistic symptoms of anxiety. The further from the truth a subject's verbal account, the more internal anxiety the subject experiences. This behavior is more likely to be relevant when observed in response to closed questions, although it can also be meaningful during other portions of the interview. Body, hand, and leg movements have meaning when observed in conjunction with responses of particular topical areas, when that behavior deviates from the behavior observed during the norming process in the rapport-building phase of the interview. It is important to stress that no particular gesture or movement is indicative of deception when seen randomly throughout the interview or even as a single isolated occurrence. The investigator must record clusters of meaningful behavior occurring around particular topical areas. Remember, lying only occurs verbally. It would be a serious error to assume that a subject who consistently avoids eye contact or engages in continuous hand or body movement is necessarily lying. It is only when these behaviors are witnessed with timing and consistency to specific questions or topical areas that they can be meaningfully interpreted. For example, if a subject who has maintained an open and frontally aligned posture throughout the interview suddenly crosses his arms and turns his body away from the interviewer before, during, or immediately after his response, this is a highly significant indicator that the subject feels uncomfortable with that particular verbal response and might be deceptive. Similarly, if a subject puts his hand over his mouth whenever discussing a particular topic during an open account, when he has not done so at any other time during the interview, that is indicative that the topic is causing him internal anxiety. Determining whether the subjects are actually lying in these examples would require the investigator to conduct further investigation.

It is easiest to examine different behaviors and their potential meanings by considering the perfect, hypothetical truthful subject and the corresponding perfect deceptive subject. The truthful subject will always sit upright and maintain a frontally-aligned and dynamic posture, he will always exhibit appropriate eye contact, employ outward or illustrative gestures, and he will lean forward when answering key questions. Truthful subjects are open and relaxed because they experience no internal anxiety and have nothing to hide. When describing a physical event, they will often use their hands to pantomime the narrative as they verbally relay the details. Their posture and degree of eye contact is dynamic, fluid, and natural, because they feel at ease. Their movements are determined solely by choice of comfort and will not reflect a pattern related to the topical issues of the interview.

In contrast, the hypothetical deceptive subject will constantly slouch, maintain an unnaturally rigid or barriered posture, engage in foot bouncing and frequent postural shifts, lack appropriate eye contact, and engage in inward or adaptive gestures. Deceptive subjects engage in barriered postures, such as crossing their arms, sitting on their hands, or partially covering their faces, because they are experiencing a degree of anxiety and symbolically do not want to let the investigator inside. They slouch because they mistakenly believe this behavior demonstrates a lack of concern, and they similarly remain frozen during an interview because they are aware that their behavior is being gauged. For the same reasons, deceptive subjects will sometimes engage in intense staring, usually only for the first few minutes of the interview, because they believe that the avoidance of eye contact is a telltale sign of deception. Their hand gestures are inward—picking lint from their sleeves, scratching their chins or ears, grooming their nails or the like—because these gestures help to relieve the internal anxiety they are feeling.

The important thing to remember is that even truthful subjects will engage in some of the so-called deceptive behaviors and visa-versa; what makes these behaviors significant is their occurrence with timing and consistency to the subject's verbal responses. For example, consider a subject who is asked the closed question, "Did you steal the money?" Assume that he has theretofore had his arms crossed throughout the interview (an example of a frozen and barriered posture), and after the question he abruptly scratches his face (an adaptive hand movement, sometimes referred to as a grooming gesture) and waits approximately three seconds to respond to the question (a latent response, given that the question does not call for memory recall or speculation). Given this conglomeration of deceptive behaviors to a very key topical question, the investigator can safely assume that the subject is lying when he responds that he did not steal the money. Still, to confirm this assumption she would need to conduct further investigation. At the very least, however, her knowledge of the subject's deception on this key point will inform her next question. It might even cause her to alter the case's hypothesis.

Another important area of evaluating deception is **paralinguistic behavior**. This behavior refers to the non-word utterances included in virtually all communication, such as sighs, coughing, laughing, clearing of the throat, and even the absence of sound (i.e., silence). Paralinguistic factors that are indicative of truthfulness include timely responses (i.e., those not deemed significantly latent) and responses where the vocal rate and pitch changes naturally when the subject discusses emotional topics. When a subject discusses a traumatic event, an investigator should expect that his rate of speech will increase and that his pitch will rise.

In contrast, deceptive responses are often significantly latent and are sometimes punctuated by non-word utterances, which constitute unintended releases of tension. Deceptive subjects also may not exhibit appropriate rate and pitch changes when discussing emotional topics. A non-word utterance, such as a laugh or a cough, is exhibited within close proximity to a significant verbal response. These are short bursts of tension relieving energy that psychologically serve to negate the statement they are associated with. Similar to the evaluation of nonverbal behavior, paralinguistic behavior is only meaningful when it is noted in conjunction with specific verbal responses. For example, a subject who exhibits a nervous laugh immediately before responding to a closed question, when he has not laughed at any other point during the interview, is experiencing a higher degree of anxiety related to that question, indicative that he may be lying in his response.

Practical exercise: With at least two other students, conduct a mock interview where one of students is the subject, one an investigator, and the third will play both the role of a client and a co-conspirator to the subject. The client/co-conspirator, who may be the class instructor, will first speak to the subject independently and instruct him to lie (or, alternatively, not to lie) about some element of his background (e.g., prior job experience) or about some event that happened to him in the recent past, and to request breaks during the interview. The client/co-

conspirator will then instruct the investigator to interview the subject about broad issue related to the lie—without disclosing to the investigator the exact nature of the lie. The investigator will then interview the subject to try to determine what he is lying about, paying particular attention to rapport; the location, setting, and length of the interview; basic questioning techniques; and the subject's verbal, nonverbal, and paralinguistic behavior. She should employ at least one admission seeking question and properly dissuade the subject from taking a break request, without creating duress. This exercise should be repeated until each student has an opportunity to play the role of both the subject and the investigator.

6

Surveillance

A common method that investigators employ to gather information is **surveillance**, which is the act of observing an unaware subject and recording his activities. The recording need not necessarily be by video, although video surveillance is the most common recording method in the private sector. Other methods include still photographs, audio recording, global positioning systems (GPS), and simple note taking. Regardless of the method used to record observations during surveillance, proper preparation is essential. An investigator must be able to recognize the subject of the surveillance and become familiar with the area surrounding his routine. Identifying the subject of the surveillance can be done by obtaining photographs from the client, or by doing online research regarding his *biometric* identifiers: ethnicity, hair color, height, weight, etc. This information can sometimes be obtained from the Department of Motor Vehicles or from court records. The investigator should also research the subject's residence, place of employment, and known associates. Placing these locations on a map shows the investigator the universe of places where the subject is likely to travel. The investigator should then review maps and online satellite images of this "universe" by accessing Google Maps, or by simply spending time driving around the area before the surveillance begins, identifying possible travel routes, vantage points, choke points and the like.

A **vantage point**, which some intelligence operatives refer to as a surveillance detection route (SDR), is an area where there is a high likelihood of surveillance detection, usually because it permits the subject to plausibly turn around or stop quickly and view what is behind him. Of course, anyone who believes they are being followed can easily lose or identify their followers by simply performing an erratic U-turn on a busy street. What a vantage point offers a subject, however, is the ability to obverse or confirm the fact that he is being observed without the investigator's knowledge. This is the worst possible outcome, because the subject may then modify his behavior during the observance. Shopping malls, traffic circles, and high-rise office buildings often provide good vantage points for subjects. A **choke point** is an area where there is only one, or at least a manageable number of routes, for a subject to travel. When setting up the surveillance, an investigator must know the choke points where the subject is likely to travel within the likely area of surveillance. Choke points include major thoroughfares, exits to buildings and parking garages, and highway entrance ramps.

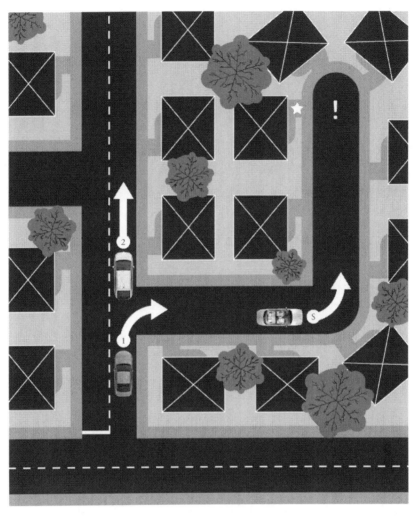

1. Investigator #1 ⭐ Subject's Home
2. Investigator #2
S. Subject ❗ Vantage Point

Cul-de-sacs where the subject has a plausible reason to be, make natural vantage points. In this diagram, the lead car (Investigator #2) should continue straight, while the second car (Investigator #1) should slow down markedly to lessen the chances the subject will spot her as she rounds the corner toward the subject's home.

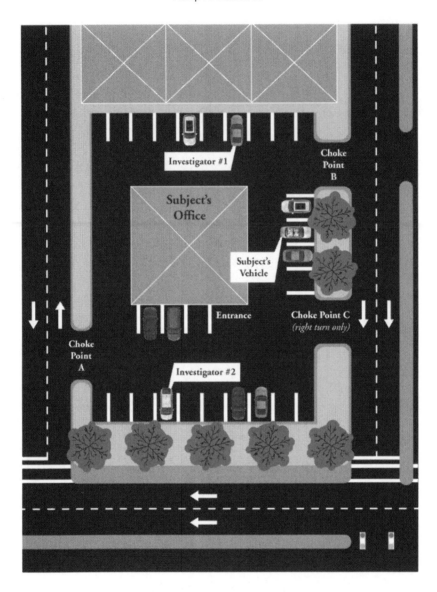

Choke points are areas where the subject must travel. In this diagram, Investigator #2 is positioned to observe the entrance of the subject's office, while Investigator #1 is positioned to observe the subject's vehicle. Tactically speaking, these are choke points in their own right. In terms of the choke points in to and out of the parking lot, the investigators are well-positioned to observe and follow the subject regardless of the route he chooses.

Before the surveillance begins, it is critical that an investigator choose a vehicle and clothing that will allow her to more easily blend in with her surroundings. Generally, dark colored clothing and vehicles garner less attention than lighter or more "flashy" attire and vehicles. The important thing to remember is that the investigator, who may be sitting in one location for hours, must look like she "belongs" there, lest a passersby come to question her, thereby drawing attention to her position, or worse yet—call the police.

Surveillance can be either covert or overt, and then either fixed or mobile. Covert surveillance involves surreptitiously observing a subject, typically from a safe distance, where the investigator cannot easily be seen by the subject, while overt surveillance involves observing the subject from a much closer distance. During overt surveillance, the investigator does not attempt to hide the fact that she is physically observing the subject, but she instead uses a ruse or cover to put the subject at ease regarding her intentions. Fixed surveillance is when an investigator remains in one location, typically observing a building or stationary structure where a subject is believed to frequent. In contrast, mobile surveillance focuses solely on a subject, irrespective of where he happens to be. Regardless of the type of surveillance an investigator is performing, the underlying theory is that, since the subject is unaware he is being observed, he will engage in his "normal" behavior, which the investigator records for purposes of testing the investigative hypothesis.

The most common type of surveillance in the private sector is **covert surveillance**, which is typically conducted in a motor vehicle, sometimes with tinted windows, or in places where the investigator can easily blend in with her surroundings, such as on foot in an area populated with retail businesses. Almost any vehicle will suffice for covert surveillance, provided that it does not stand out too much on the road. Anything that draws attention to the vehicle, such as unusual color schemes, bumper stickers and the like, is a detriment to a successful surveillance operation because it increases the chances that a subject will notice the vehicle *twice* and thereby recognize that he is being followed. Even tinted windows are a double-edged sword, because they cause the surveillance vehicle to "fit the profile" of a vehicle that might be used to conduct surveillance. Windows that are darkly tinted also drastically degrade the quality of video footage taken at night. It is important that an investigator recognize that the subject being observed typically has no idea that he is being watched. It is therefore best to remain as calm and natural as possible. For example, while hunkering down in a dark-colored van with tinted windows might make an investigator feel more secure that she will not be seen by the subject, such a vehicle, observed from the outside, is bound to be viewed as an anomaly by most casual observers and perhaps even by the subject, thereby drawing unexpected and unwanted attention.

In contrast to covert surveillance, an investigator conducting **overt surveillance** is not at all concerned about being observed by the subject. In the security industry, overt surveillance includes video security cameras, which are typically placed in plain sight. Probation and parole agencies sometimes employ ankle bracelets to monitor the whereabouts of the subjects they are tasked with monitoring. This is also an example of overt surveillance. Although it is common knowledge that the purpose of these cameras and ankle bracelets is to conduct surveillance, subjects sometimes become desensitized to their presence and continue performing nefarious deeds while their behavior is being observed and recorded. However, the primary difference between overt surveillance in the investigative and security industries is that security surveillance is often intended to modify a subject's behavior, under the theory that people who believe they are being observed will not steal or abscond from justice. From an investigator's standpoint, overt surveillance must not tip off the subject that the surveillance is of any consequence. In other words, the last thing an investigator wants to do is modify a subject's behavior, as this taints the purpose of observance in the first place. The surveillance therefore must seem wholly natural and completely nonthreatening. This is sometimes also referred to as conducting an undercover investigation.

An investigator conducting an undercover investigation or overt surveillance is like an actor playing a role in a live "theatre" with no script. It requires exceptional skill and quick thinking, where the slightest mistake or hesitation can jeopardize the entire investigation. Sometimes an investigator engaged in covert surveillance will also go undercover to get close to a subject who has gone into an area impossible to observe covertly. For example, while conducting a covert surveillance, if a subject walks into an apartment building, an investigator might follow the subject onto the elevator and casually introduce herself as a new neighbor to try to glean what the subject is doing there. Typically, the more simple and natural the cover story, the more successful an overt operation will be. Often undercover investigations are conducted for a very specific purpose and are very short in duration, although they can also be incredibly elaborate and last for months. The key to such cases is to practice the cover story thoroughly and to act naturally. Similar to covert surveillance, most subjects do not expect the observation of an overt operative.

Surveillance is fixed when the investigator remains in one place. Although the place might be a building or other structure, in the private sector it is more often a vehicle that simply remains stationary. **Fixed surveillance** is useful for observing what happens at a particular location, irrespective of any subjects coming or going from that location. Because an investigator staying in one location for a long period of time tends to arise suspicion, fixed surveillance is most effective when conducted from a place where the investigator is unlikely to be seen at all, or when the surveillance is actually overt, such as when an investigator pretends to have broken down, employs a utility van, or the like. One trick to avoid suspicion when seated in a vehicle during fixed surveillance is to sit in the vehicle's passenger seat. A person sitting in the driver's seat of a car that is not moving seems unnatural. It also limits suspicions to keep the vehicle turned away from the focus of the surveillance and to use the mirrors for indirect observation.

In contrast, **mobile surveillance** involves following a subject wherever he may go. It begins when the subject is "picked up," typically at a location where it is known he will be in advance. Depending on the reliability of the intelligence that determined the likely pick-up point, sometimes an investigator will have to remain in this location for quite some time before the subject finally arrives—if he arrives at all. This type of surveillance may be by vehicle or on foot, but is usually the former. Foot surveillance is fundamentally the same as vehicular surveillance and is often performed in concert with vehicular surveillance, such as when a subject drives to a locale and then exits his vehicle. The biggest obstacle to successful mobile surveillance is traffic, because it is exceedingly difficult and dangerous to follow a subject unseen without interference from other motorists, traffic lights, and pedestrians. These difficulties are compounded for novice investigators who do not know the correct lead distance to afford a subject without arousing his suspicion about the surveillance or losing sight of him due to traffic. The proper lead distance varies widely depending on the location of the surveillance. In the city, an investigator should tail a subject from no further than half a block, decreasing that distance to no less than three car lengths when approaching an intersection with a traffic light, and then retreating to a half-block distance once she crosses the intersection. In the suburbs and in rural areas, an investigator may sometimes allow the distance to reach to 150 yards on straight roads, but always decreasing the distance when the subject approaches a major intersection. This is intended to prevent the investigator from losing the subject at a red light or in the event that the subject makes two successive turns before the investigator reaches the intersection.

Because of these difficulties, mobile surveillance is easier with multiple investigators who may follow the subject more closely than a solitary investigator (sometimes within a car length in the city) and not arise any suspicion by periodically interchanging their positions. The more investigators on a surveillance team, the closer they can follow without arising suspicion, and consequently the less chance they have of losing the subject in traffic. Whenever using multiple investigators, it is important they remain in constant contact with each other via radio. Unfortunately, using multiple investigators is cost-prohibitive for many clients in the private sector.

A subject who suspects that he is being followed will sometimes perform an erratic maneuver, such as a breakneck turn, intended to test the investigator. If the investigator follows the subject by making a similar, sudden turn, then she will be identified as a tail by the subject. Investigators refer to this as being burned. It is always best for the investigator to remain calm and not be baited into trying to follow an erratic subject. If a subject performs such an erratic maneuver, and it is reasonably believed that he is aware or suspects that he is being followed, the investigator should cease the surveillance and resume on another day—next time with more operatives. However, it is important to note that many motorists drive erratically as their normal behavior, so such behavior does not necessarily mean the investigation is in jeopardy.

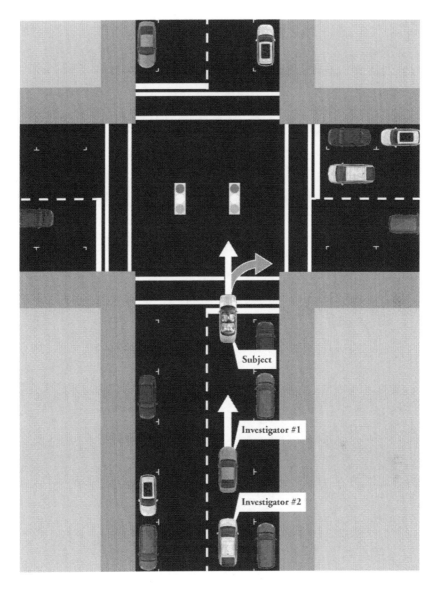

In this diagram, the arrows show two possible directions where the subject may go at an intersection.

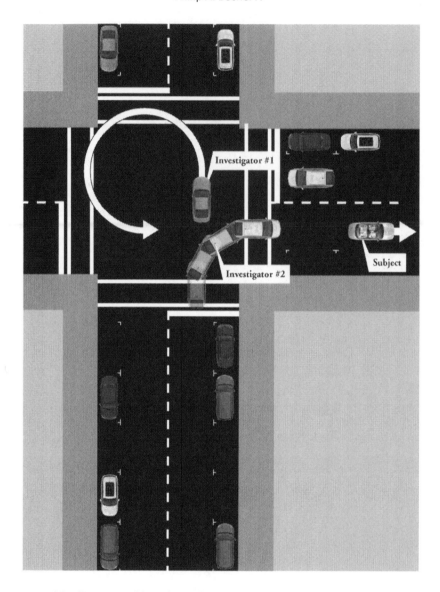

In this diagram, the subject has made a right turn at the intersection. Investigator #1 relinquishes the eyeball to Investigator
#2, and then makes a broad U-turn to take a position behind In-
vestigator #2. The subject will not be suspicious of Investigator
#2's car, and will perceive Investigator #1's car—assuming that
he perceives it at all—as having turned onto the road from the
opposite direction from which he came.

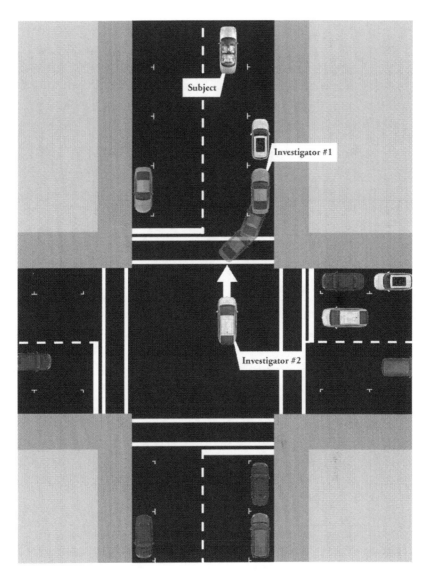

In this diagram, the subject has traveled straight through the intersection. This time, Investigator #1 simply pulls momentarily behind a parked car, allowing Investigator #2 to pull ahead and take the eyeball. After Investigator #2's car passes, Investigator #1 will pull back onto the road and assume the tailing position.

In terms of documenting the subject's behavior during surveillance, private investigators typically use a digital video camera with night vision for covert surveillance, and a pinhole camera coupled with an audio recording device for overt surveillance (and for covert surveillance conducted in highly populated places). When employing a video camera, it is customary among private investigators to record a set-up shot that simply pans the area where the surveillance will occur. The set-up shot is a sound business practice meant to establish, in the event that the surveillance turns up no meaningful evidence, that the investigator was at the location when she claimed to be. Sometimes investigators also record a closing shot for this same purpose.

Some investigators employ GPS devices that may be attached to the undercarriage of a subject's vehicle to track the vehicle's movement either in real time or by polling the vehicle's movement over a longer duration of time, creating interval snapshots of where the vehicle has traveled. After the U.S. Supreme Court's decision in *United States v. Jones*,[11] GPS devices are now only legal with a warrant or with the consent of the vehicle's owner, meaning that private investigators must obtain the consent of the owner before installing a GPS device to track another subject driving the vehicle. Some states, following the *Jones* decision, sought to clarify the rules related to GPS trackers by passing their own laws. In Virginia, for example, private investigators are now also prevented from using GPS devices for clients who are under protective orders, or where there is reason to believe the information obtained may be used in commission of a crime.[12] The fact that private investigators must obtain the vehicle owner's consent in order to legally employ GPS trackers practically limits their use to domestic surveillance cases, and cases where employers are investigating employees who are using company vehicles.

Another important element to remember regarding the recording method used during surveillance is that the information gathered during surveillance is evidence, and must therefore be competent in order to be admissible in court. This means, for example, that the quality of the video footage matters a great deal, and that every piece of evidence must be meticulously documented and stored. For example, an investigator shooting video footage should always use both hands to steady the camera or otherwise brace the camera against a stationary object during filming to avoid jumpiness. Monopods work well for this purpose, as they allow the investigator to hold the camera steady while not being as cumbersome as a tripod. Likewise, if filming from a vehicle, the investigator should make sure that her windows are clean of dirt and debris that could hamper the quality of the video. The procedures for properly documenting evidence will be discussed in greater detail in Part III (Documentation).

It is common for private investigators conducting covert surveillance to be approached by law enforcement or concerned citizens about their activity. The best way to deal with the inquiries of citizens is to have a simple cover story prepared in advance, such as, "I am waiting for a friend." A private investigator is not required to display her identification or to disclose the fact that she is conducting an investigation at the request of a private citizen. In fact, since the investigator has no way of knowing whether the citizen will tip off the subject about the surveillance, an investigator should never discuss the fact that she is conducting an investigation with a private citizen. In some states (e.g., Virginia) a private investigator is required to display her registration card at the request of a law enforcement officer, but she is not required to disclose the identity of her client or the subject, or to otherwise provide details of her investigation. Because police cars have the potential to draw attention to the investigator and jeopardize her case, it is best to be forthcoming with police officers so they will leave the area as quickly as possible.

One useful tactic when conducting fixed, vehicular surveillance is to sit in the passenger seat and position the vehicle facing away from the subject. This draws less attention to the investigator, who can observe activity behind her using the car's mirrors. When recording video becomes necessary, she can swivel her body around in the seat, focus the camera out of the rear window, and use the car's seat to steady the shot.

Practical exercise: With at least two other students, assign one student to be the subject and the others to be investigators. The investigators should prepare a dossier on the subject using what is known and using available public records, mapping out the likely scene of the surveillance including choke points and vantage points. Practice setting up and conducting mobile, covert surveillance, both with vehicles and on foot. Have the subject lead the investigators into different environments and practice working in teams, remaining the proper distance from the subject.

Conclusion

Part II discussed how to conduct research, interviews, and surveillance, and demonstrated how successfully solving problems requires a system of investigation like the scientific method. Conducting investigations means having a clearly identified problem, a hypothesis with which to test solutions to the problem, and the requisite know-how regarding how to investigate the evidence that can solve the problem. Testing a hypothesis may be accomplished by database research; interviewing and interpreting a subject's behavioral symptoms of deception; and/or covert or overt surveillance. Which tools an investigator employs in her investigative toolbox during any given case depends wholly on the problem, and on other external constraints placed on the investigation, such as budgets and legal considerations. Having a disciplined and systematic method of problem solving should be a universal skillset for all investigators, regardless of the method of investigation used in any particular case.

Notes

1. Perron, Brandan (1998). *"Uncovering Reasonable Doubt."* Investigative Support Specialist: Florida.

2. The federal Drivers Privacy Protection Acct, 18 U.S. Code § 2721 et seq., has an exception carved out for licensed private investigators to the general prohibition on states disclosing drivers' information to third parties.

3. *McBurney v. Young,* 133 S. Ct. 421 – 2012

4. Schlein, A.M. (2003). *Find It Online: The Complete Guide to Online Research.* Facts on Demand Press; Tempe, Arizona.

5. Ibid.

6. See Chapter 2 concerning the ethics of misrepresentation and undercover investigations.

7. It is important to note that much of my early knowledge of interviewing and interrogation was learned through the many courses I took with John E. Reid & Associates (www.reid.com). However, since I have personally conducted thousands of interviews and read countless books on behavioral analysis, my knowledge has somewhat taken on a life of its own, spurred by these early pioneers. Still, many of my concepts regarding interviewing discussed herein were sparked by my training in the Reid Method, in which I am certified, and I must give them credit for helping me formulate my ideas. The distinctions between an interview and an interrogation, for example, are drawn directly from the Reid material.

8. Code of Virginia, Sections 54.1-1800 through 54.1-1805

9. Employee Polygraph Protection Act of 1988, 29 U.S.C. § 2001

10. Buckley, W. & Jayne, B. (1999). *The Investigator's Anthology.* John E. Reid & Associates; Chicago, IL.

11. *United States v. Jones*, 565 U.S.132, 2012

12. Code of Virginia § 18.2-60.5

Part III
Documentation

7

Managing the Investigation

You can piece together seemingly tangential clues to solve a complex and disjointed investigation like Sherlock Holmes, but if you cannot adequately convey the results of the investigation in a timely, concise, and clear manner, then you cannot be an effective investigator. The evidence uncovered during an investigation is only valuable once it is given to the client, and then only if it is admissible in a court proceeding. This means that an investigator should be preparing to testify from the minute she begins working on a case and should conduct her investigation accordingly. It also means that she should recognize her business is contingent upon the satisfaction of her clients. Proper record and time keeping are just as important as finding the solution to a case's stated problem. If the case was documented properly, testifying should not be a major concern, and the business model of providing investigative services for a fee will be sustainable. Conducting a thorough investigation and engaging in sound business and investigative practices from the beginning will directly influence the degree to which an investigator will be comfortable and compelling on the stand—and the extent to which her company will profit from her services.

Case Initiation, Billing, and Testimony

In private investigations, a case begins when the firm is hired by a client. A client will generally be a law firm, a private company, or another investigative firm, although it may simply be a private citizen willing to pay for lawfully gathered information. The fee, terms, and scope of work are agreed upon, and the investigative firm then sets about conducting the investigation until its conclusion or until the client decides to stop the investigation. The leading reasons why clients decide to stop investigations are that they have either run out of funds or the information gathered during the early stages of the investigation has not been fruitful (has not supported the clients' hoped-for hypothesis). This does not reflect negatively on the investigator; it is the nature of the business that clients' expectations may not comport with the evidence.

From the investigative firm's standpoint, a case is not considered closed until all of its assigned tasks have been completed and the client requests no further action. It is critical that all major events in a case are documented, including the suspension or termination of an investigation. For example, if all tasks in a case have been completed but the case is still pending payment of services or a legal outcome—including the possibility of future testimony—or if it remains open pending any further developments, a task describing the circumstances and important dates in the case must be maintained in the task tracking system by the case manager or lead investigator. The running resume for the case (discussed below) must then be updated to include the reason for the case being effectively terminated.

To keep track of time spent working a case for billing purposes, investigative companies should use an Internet based software program that integrates their billing into accounting and payroll software, and automatically generates an invoice that is sent to the client each month. Many companies borrow their billing systems from law firms, using tenth-of-an-hour increments to express the individual tasks they perform for clients. Other companies use quarters-of-an-hour, and some companies may use flat rates or even real time. Tenth-of-an-hour systems follow the chart provided, where each billable task that falls within the minute column is billed according to its corresponding decimal.

Minutes	Decimal
1-6	.1
7-12	.2
13-18	.3
19-24	.4
25-30	.5
31-36	.6
37-42	.7
43-48	.8
49-54	.9
55-60	1.0

Investigative tasks that take longer than an hour to complete are expressed with a whole number. For example, one hour and twenty-three minutes would be expressed as 1.4, etc. It is not uncommon for investigators to maintain their times on a handwritten form or in an Excel spreadsheet. What is important to note is that, similar to the legal profession, it is standard practice for investigators to detail all their work in a line-by-line format. While this process is sometimes very tedious for novice investigators, it eventually becomes second nature. The better records an investigator keeps about her time and activities, the less likely a client will question those charges when he receives the invoice for services rendered.

In terms of what to do with documents after a case has been concluded, many states require companies to maintain a copy of client contracts. In Virginia, the Department of Criminal Justice Services requires private investigation firms to keep such records for a period of three years from the completion of the agreement, but they do not regulate the amount of time that an investigative firm must maintain records concerning the substantive investigation. However, it is a sound business practice to maintain these files for *at least* five years after the case is closed. For cases that went to trial, if there is even a remote chance for an appeal, then the corresponding records should be kept indefinitely until there is no chance they will be needed.

Expectations, Clear Instructions, and Chain of Command

Besides the need to prepare for testimony and the need to recoup money from the client, evidence must be documented before it becomes actionable in the investigation itself. Improper documentation necessarily leads to mismanagement and risks case failure. It is critical to prepare frequent status reports, respond to all requests for updates, and maintain active task lists to ensure that no investigative tasks slip through the cracks. If the investigator is working with other investigators or as part of a larger legal team, as is regularly the case, she must schedule regular meetings to discuss and coordinate tasks so that everyone knows their role and responsibilities.

When delegating instructions, it is always preferable to have a written record so the designee will later be able to reference the details of the task that may be lost in a verbal directive. This method may not always be practical given the urgency of a particular task. Whether the instructions are verbal or written, they must be inclusive of all information that is necessary to perform the task. An investigator should never assume that someone else knows everything she knows. In issuing clear instructions, it is helpful to reiterate an understanding of who is to perform which tasks, and what contingent plans will be enacted in the event that a particular task cannot be performed as planned. When receiving instructions, the investigator must ensure that she fully understands what is being asked of her, and she should ask for clarification if something in unclear. Also, she should ask about contingency instructions in the event that something does not occur as expected.

When an investigator is working with others, there must be one person who takes primary responsibility for the task at hand. This person is typically referred to as the case's lead investigator. Leaving this authority and responsibility ambiguous is a recipe for finger-pointing and fruitless blaming when something goes wrong. When an investigator assigns authority, she needs to make this chain of command clear to the others in the group so there will be no misunderstandings or resentment. She must also make it clear to the designated assignee that he is ultimately responsible for the actions of those beneath him. This practice applies to all groups, regardless of size. Once authority is granted and responsibility implicitly accepted, trust must be bestowed on that person (e.g., the assigned investigator) to further structure the group as he sees fit, as he is now ultimately responsible for that task's success or failure.

In practice, it is best that all new cases be approved by a principal or owner of the investigative company. The principal should be responsible for obtaining a signed contract and retainer, if required, at which point the case can be assigned to a lead investigator. Retainers serve two purposes and should be required of all but a firm's most regular and trusted clients. First, by collecting fees prior to services, an investigative firm is assured timely payment for its services. Secondly, a retainer protects against conflicts of interest, because, in the event that representation ceases before completion of the investigation (i.e., before available funds are used up), the firm may keep the retainer without fear of losing income after being prohibited from working on a subsequent case due to a conflict of interest—because they have already been paid in full for the first case.

After receiving the signed contract and depositing the retainer, the principal will be responsible for briefing the lead investigator about the case, the client-specific protocol to follow, the investigative strategy to be taken, and the budget, if any. The lead investigator (or case manager, if applicable) will then be responsible for all contact with the client, and for conducting the tactical investigation on the case, including the coordination of those tasks assigned to other investigators in the firm. The assigning principal will be thereafter copied on all further emails and communication with the client. The lead investigator will also be responsible for establishing a digital file on the company's internal server by creating an appropriate root file in the active cases directory, typically of the representing law firm or client-company, and creating a client-specific folder. Within that folder the lead investigator should create the appropriate subfolders designated by the company's protocol, such as subfolders for draft reports, final reports, case documents and the like.

After a case is accepted and assigned, individual investigative tasks will either originate from the principal, the lead investigator, or the client directly. All tasks generally fall first into one of two broad categories. The first are those that require an investigative report, which will be sent (after an internal review) directly to the client upon completion of the task. Even if the task cannot be completed, the assigned investigator will still generate and send a report outlining any efforts made and the specific reasons why the task could not be completed.

The second category of tasks exists when a client requests that an investigative report not be generated, or when a principal decides that a task does not require the generation of an investigative report. For this second type of task, a brief but detailed notation should still be added in that case's **running resume** for tracking purposes. A running resume is a shared document or software system, similar to a journal, where investigators working on a given case provide brief status updates concurrent with each effort made to complete the case's individual tasks. The running resume should be maintained by the firm and may or may not be shared with the client, as decided by a principal on a case by case basis. There is no specific requirement to offer a case's running resume to a client, but it can, upon closing an investigation, be easily modified to become the concluding report. A running resume must include sufficient detail of the individual notations—including exact times and environmental data. It thus allows the principal and lead investigator to easily check on the status of each active investigation, and also provides assurance that each task is being performed to the company's standards.

Typically, all interviews and surveillance will automatically be designated as tasks requiring the completion of a formal investigative report, unless directed otherwise by a principal. Research requires a report only when the goal of the research is the end goal of the given task. For example, research only to locate a witness so that he may be interviewed does not necessarily require a report, since that witness's whereabouts would be included in the report concerning the interview. If the completion of such a task is hindered, either due to budget limitations or other circumstances, the lead investigator must inform the principal or the case manager, depending on the company's protocol, and provide details of this development. If the principal, after discussing the matter with the client, then deems that the task is no longer necessary, the investigator responsible for the task must complete an investigative report detailing the substantive accomplishments or what efforts were made to complete the task. The investigator must additionally add a notation to the running resume referencing that a report was generated in relation to the task. An example of such a running resume entry example might be:

> The investigator arrived at 5800 Pennsylvania Ave., NW, at approximately 14:05 to interview Stephanie JONES, and a white woman in her 50s answered the door and said that she recently moved into the home and did not know anyone named "Stephanie." She added that "Stephanie" could have been one of the daughters of the couple who moved out last month. See status report titled, "2013_07_03_Jones Stephanie location."

During the initiation of a case, the principal and client should discuss in specific detail who is to be the recipient of completed investigative reports and ongoing case email correspondence. This list will include any attorneys or other clients who are to receive the reports, as well as any additional contacts, including, but not limited to, legal assistants, interns, or outside investigators. These steps are important in order to avoid communication lapses or misdirected reports to the client.

> **Discussion:** Why is preparing to testify from the beginning of an investigation essential in our profession? What are the three general methods of tracking billable investigative time? What are the pros and cons of each method? What is the purpose of a contract and retainer? Why is the chain of command so important during an investigation? What is the purpose of a running resume?

8

The Products of Investigation

Real Evidence

With a sound process of managing an investigation in effect, an investigator may then concentrate her attention on the act of actually collecting and documenting evidence for her investigation. Some means of documenting evidence are written statements, video recordings, still photographs, diagrams, and sketches. In addition to documenting evidence, investigators may also secure real evidence directly. When gathering evidence, the investigator must be concerned about its integrity, and this is especially true regarding the collection of real evidence. The integrity of evidence relates to its competence. Because the primary goal of an investigation is to gather evidence, the way in which real evidence is collected and preserved has a direct bearing on whether the evidence will be admissible at trial. Although evidence gathered may be real, testimonial, or demonstrative, it is primarily with real evidence where its competence is most often called into question. Even when real evidence is found to be competent by a judge and is admitted into evidence, it is often impeached based on its presumed lack of competence by the opposition. Proper documentation is critical to ensuring the evidence is highly competent and remains unimpeachable.

The first consideration regarding the competence of real evidence is the protection of the scene. The **theory of transfer** holds that a suspect always leaves something at a crime scene and always takes something away. The theory is equally applicable to real evidence gathered in civil investigations. Contamination occurs when evidence is added, removed, or changed in any manner from the way in which it was found by the investigator. As such, the investigator must take great care to protect the scene from all outside contamination including the addition of extraneous fingerprints and DNA.

Finger prints may either be latent prints or patent. **Latent prints** are left on many surfaces by the oils and amino acids secreted by a person's skin. They can survive on paper for decades and are typically extracted with special methods, including iodine fuming, silver nitrate solutions, and ninhydrin spray. **Patent prints** are the result of foreign substances (e.g., paint or blood). How long these prints remain depends on the makeup of the foreign substance. In the event there is physical evidence that could conceivably be submitted for later forensic analysis, the investigator should always wear gloves and avoid handling evidence in a way that will complicate or undermine the subsequent analysis.

Before anything is altered at the scene, still photographs should be taken of every conceivable angle and every conceivable detail in a coordinated series, from general to specific. A measurement marker, such as a ruler, can be used to photograph small items, although a second photograph should also be taken of the same item without the marker. All photographs should be linked to the identity and specific location of the subject; the identity of the photographer; the identifying case number, if applicable; the specific time the photograph was taken; and data to describe the weather conditions, photographic equipment, and printing methods. Because it is normally impractical to mark the photograph itself with this information (especially in the case of digital images) the investigator should prepare a report that contains this information each time she takes a series of photographs. The same basic rules apply to video evidence, although instead of several photographs there will be only one digital video file. It is standard when taking investigative video footage to begin with a setup shot of the general area. With video, it is important to maintain a steady camera so the footage will be of good quality and not overly confusing. Using a monopod or tripod is recommended for this purpose. The investigator should also keep in mind that most video cameras contain an audio component, so what she says during the recording may be discoverable later in court, depending on the type of case and its jurisdiction. Therefore, she should watch what she says at all times.

It is important to note that all images uncovered during investigations, whether stills or videos, are highly subject to manipulation, both intentionally and unintentionally. Great care should be taken by the investigator to ensure that each image is as close to the objective reality as possible. Therefore, avoid using extreme angles to make an object appear larger or smaller, farther away, etc. Degrees of lightness and darkness are also highly susceptible to manipulation. For example, the appearance of light can be radically controlled by using differing film speeds or adjusting the shutter speed or aperture. With digital cameras, the potential for manipulation is even easier, and it is now possible with readily available software to radically alter images. Investigators should only capture images that fairly and accurately represent the object or objects they are intended to record—and it is never appropriate to alter an image in any way to make it appear more helpful to the case. However, it is allowable, under certain circumstances, to enhance an image, such as for purposes of identifying a subject. When enhancing an image, it is important to retain a copy of the original, unaltered image, and to include in the report exactly what steps were taken to enhance the image. An investigator may be called to follow the same steps under an examination to show that the image was not substantively changed, but only enhanced. It is also prudent to test all equipment, such as the batteries, amount of memory or film, etc., well prior to conducting the investigation.

After taking photographs during the collection of real evidence, investigators should consider drawing a sketch, preferably in scale to the actual locale. Items of relevance may be measured via triangulation, the rectangular coordinate method, or the straight-line method. **Triangulation** is when two fixed points are chosen, and two distances are measured to a given item of investigative interest. By knowing the whereabouts of the two fixed objects and the direction and distances to the object in question, an investigator can state exactly where the object was recovered. This method is convenient for measuring objects in outdoor crime or accident scenes. The **rectangular coordinate method** is used for indoor scenes or any time that there are two walls (or similar structures) that meet at a right angle. By measuring the distance to each wall from the object in a straight line and forming a right angle, the investigator can pinpoint where the object was found within the room in relation to the two walls. The **straight-line method** is used to measure objects that are located along a wall. A corner, door, or other fixed point is chosen along the wall, and the investigator simply takes a measurement from that location to the object in question. For long outdoor distances, it is helpful to use a measuring wheel.

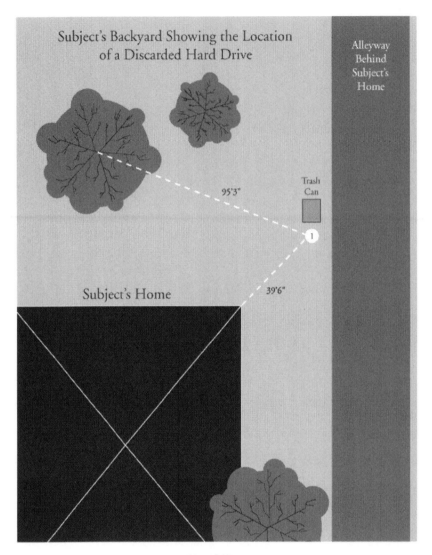

1. Hard Drive

This diagram shows how an investigator can use triangulation to document where she found a discarded hard drive near a subject's home.

CONFERENCE ROOM SHOWING LOCATION OF
SURREPTITIOUS SURVELLANCE DEVICES DISCOVERED ON 10/1/03
(Exploded View)

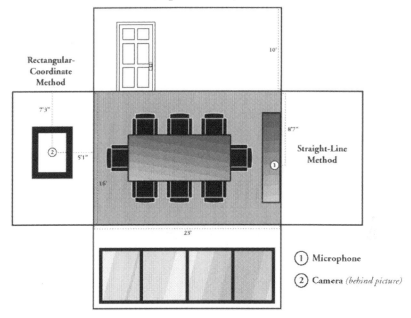

This exploded diagram shows how an investigator might employ the rectangular coordinate method and the straight-line method to illustrate where she discovered illegal recording devices in a client's conference room. An exploded diagram, which is a way of depicting a room in three dimensions, is drawn with the walls folded outward, like a dismantled shoe box.

Before collecting any evidence, the investigator should take notes detailing the specific time an item was found; the exact location where it was found; the name of the investigator who located the evidence; a description of the item; and the names of anyone present when the item was located and secured. Notes are very important during the different stages of an investigation because it is nearly impossible to document findings in real time with anything resembling an official report. By taking notes contemporaneously with the collection of real evidence (or while conducting interviews or fixed surveillance), the investigator can be sure that the facts match her recollection. Likewise, notes buttress an investigator's credibility in the eyes of those later tasked with assessing the viability of the case's conclusion.

During the collection of real evidence, large and obvious items should be collected first, followed by smaller items. Gloves or tweezers should be used so as not to contaminate the evidence with the investigator's fingerprints or DNA. Evidence should be packaged in clean, separate containers, sealed tightly to protect against contamination, and inscribed by the investigator who secured it for future identification. Evidence should then be kept in a locked room or file cabinet, if possible, and a log created to continually track its whereabouts. To ensure competence, all evidence must be properly accounted for from the moment it is seized until it is presented in court. This is termed the **chain of custody**. A simple sign-in/sign-out sheet will typically suffice, with a column for the signatures of investigators and others who handled the evidence, and another column to record the date and time the evidence was received.

Practical Exercise: Place a small object (e.g., a stapler) in a room or somewhere outside. This object now represents a gun, knife, or some other object relevant to an investigation. Keeping the theory of transfer in mind, carefully photograph, sketch, and diagram the exact location where the evidence was "found" by using one of the three methods of measuring crime scene distances. If time allows, the object should be collected and packaged, and a chain of custody log created for its future handling.

Notes and Reports

It is not always feasible to prepare reports or add to a case's running resume while out in the field. Therefore, the first practical application of documenting any type of evidence during an investigation typically starts with taking notes. In short, an investigator should take notes about everything she does, from securing real evidence, conducting interviews, and even surveillance. Practically speaking, she may not always be able to take notes during an activity, such as during a mobile surveillance or during an interview with a non-cooperative witness, but she should jot down everything she recalls promptly after the fact to maintain a clear record of the event. Sometimes investigators opt to maintain records during mobile surveillance by using an audio recording device, which is acceptable, provided there is a system in place to store these audio files for later review. An investigator must always use a clean sheet of paper and include the date regarding each separate event. Notes are typically not turned over to clients, but they may become discoverable by the opposition in some instances, especially if the investigator has to testify about the underlying incident, so it is important that notes never call into question the investigator's recollection of the event. If notes are conducted during an interview or surveillance, it is prudent for her to review them afterward and clean them up while her memory is still fresh about the events that transpired. Notes taken in a haphazard manner may be confusing or appear contradictory to a subsequent report, which can negatively affect the case if the notes are later deemed discoverable. Most investigators develop their own particular shorthand that saves them time in the field but makes the events clear when writing their reports.

If notes are the bridge to reports, then reports are the single most important product of any investigation; the primary tangible work product of the entire case. While other evidence sometimes rivals the importance of reports, such as a particularly compelling video tape, the report is necessary to provide context to that evidence. A good report necessarily details the progress and the ultimate outcome of the investigation in a way that is meaningful to the client or others reading the report. It also provides a lasting record of the investigation that can be referenced even years later. There are generally three types of reports: preliminary reports, status reports, and concluding reports.

Preliminary reports may be prepared by a principal, the case manager, or the lead investigator, but more often in the private sector the client prepares the preliminary report. This is typically an email outlining the nature of the investigation, and may implicitly include the case's goal or problem that needs to be solved. The preliminary report may not be a report at all, and it may not even be written down, as many clients prefer to relay directions verbally. In more complicated investigations, a principal may sit down with the client and subsequently generate a preliminary report that acts as a memorandum of understanding regarding what the client hopes will be accomplished during the investigation.

Next, a **status report** is the most common type of report, documenting every individual action taken during the course of an investigation, including every interview, attempted interview, and every instance of surveillance or research. Exactly when to generate a status report is determined by the company's protocol and by perceived need, but generally status reports are generated any time an investigative task has been completed. For status reports intended to document failures, the investigator may draw largely from the notes and from the case's running resume for details of efforts taken to complete the task.

Concluding reports are more common in larger investigations than smaller ones because status reports often do an adequate job explaining the results of less complicated investigations. In larger investigations, concluding reports are necessary to tie all the relevant facts contained in the many status reports together into a single comprehensive report. One way to generate a concluding report is to simply polish the case's running resume and provide to the client as an ongoing account of the entire investigation from start to finish. Coupled with the task-specific status reports, the running resume should include everything the client needs to know about the results of the investigation and the efforts taken to obtain those results.

The typical format of an investigative report includes a summary in the beginning, followed by a detailed narrative of the findings, with a conclusion at the end. However, some companies prepare memos concerning interviews without a conclusion, and with the body of the memo substantively verbatim and chronological as to the given investigative task. The important requirement is that the report must be understandable to someone not involved in the case, and that it be an accurate representation of the finding and a narrative of how the investigation occurred. Also, reports should always include the necessary contextual data, such as case name, date, name of the author, and the names of all recipients of the report. The investigator should avoid using investigative jargon in the report, and should not write the report in the third person, except within the running resume.

It is critical that all reports describe the facts fairly and accurately, and remain as objective as possible. An investigator should never embellish facts, but it is also important that she be conscious of the tendency among novice investigators to either infer facts that were merely implied or to inadvertently imply facts or circumstances that are not clearly established by the evidence. One way to ensure accuracy is for the investigator to learn how to clearly recognize the distinction between an opinion that summarizes a set of facts and the facts themselves, and to never provide an opinion about the issue under investigation. For example, the statement that a witness lied is an *opinion*, and it would be inappropriate to make this statement in any investigative report. However, the specific, observed behaviors that inclined the investigator to believe that the subject was lying (e.g., a factual contradiction or a latent response) might be legitimately included in a report.

During an interview, an investigator must also carefully differentiate facts from the opinions of others. She must distinguish between those facts that a witness personally *knows* from the witness's opinions disguised as facts. Often these opinions are based on nothing more than hearsay. By asking questions during the interview that establish a witness's basis of opinion, it is often possible to identify the observable facts that led the witness to that opinion. For example, if a witness describes a person as "angry"—clearly an opinion—the investigator might then ask him to describe the behaviors that led him to his belief that the person was angry. This basis of belief may be built upon legitimate, observable facts, such as the person having a raised voice or being "red faced." In the above example, without the establishment of the basis of belief—e.g., that the person had a raised voice and a red face—the fact that the witness merely believed the person was angry is otherwise an unsubstantiated opinion.

All investigative reports should be reviewed for spelling mistakes, punctuation errors, and unclear wording by a principal, the case manager, lead investigator, or an editor employed for that purpose. However, when these options are unavailable, a principal may approve another investigator or staff employee to review and edit the report, and, if needed, send it to the client. The names of each reviewer should be included in the report, and all changes made to the report should be carefully tracked. This level of transparency is vital because the opposition may later claim that the original report was substantially altered, calling into question the evidence as detailed in the report. After the report has been reviewed and edited, the reviewer should save the marked document to the appropriate subfolder. Any changes that are not simple spelling, grammar, or clarity corrections must be approved by the authoring investigator. Anything that may be unclear and not immediately apparent to the reviewer should be referred to the author of the report for clarification. An example of an ambiguous, unclear report entry is the following:

*When asked if Larry MICHAELS ever mentioned Jane SMITH's death to his co-workers, JONES said that it was odd how MICHAELS mentioned that SMITH's parents **did** (emphasis added) just one month earlier.*

In the previous example, when, after contacting the author, it is determined that MICHAELS was referring to the death of SMITH's parents, the report should be rewritten as:

> When asked if Larry MICHAELS ever mentioned Jane SMITH's death to his co-workers, JONES said that it was odd how MICHAELS mentioned that SMITH's parents **died** (emphasis added) just one month earlier.

In the first example, the simple absence of the letter "e" in "died" completely alters the account of what the witness told the interviewing investigator. Reviewers should never, however, change anything substantive in quotations without first clearing the change with the report's author. Once the report has been reviewed and finalized, the draft should be maintained electronically, and the final version should be converted to an Adobe Acrobat .pdf or a similarly immutable format and placed in the appropriate subfolder. That final file should then be forwarded to the investigator who composed it, or to the case manager or lead investigator for delivery to the client.

> **Discussion:** What is the theory of transfer? Why is it so important to take notes during an investigation? What is the purpose and typical format of an investigative report? How can an investigator ensure that a report is fair and accurate, and that it clearly differentiates between fact and opinion?

Statements

Other documentary evidence frequently collected by investigators include statements, affidavits, and declarations. The terms are not mutually exclusive—affidavits or declarations, for example, are essentially types of statements—but from a practical standpoint the format and method in which the documents are collected are fundamentally different. The overarching purpose of all statements, whether affidavits, declarations, or otherwise, is to perpetuate testimony and memory. The principle difference between **affidavits** and **declarations** is that an affidavit must be signed and sworn to before a notary public, while declarations do not require a notary seal. Investigators may find it useful to become licensed notaries in the jurisdictions where they routinely work in order to create affidavits. However, state and federal law generally allows declarations into evidence in most instances. The procedures for obtaining sworn declarations are fundamentally the same as for obtaining affidavits.

What differentiates a statement from a declaration or an affidavit is its format. What investigators are typically referring to when they say "statement" is a **verbatim statement** taken from a witness immediately following an interview. In contrast, declarations and affidavits are obtained after reviewing the investigative report concerning an interview and asking the witness to sign an abbreviated statement, called a declaration or an affidavit, that only addresses the specific evidence relevant to the case. The choice of which type of statement to use will depend upon the perceived degree of cooperation by the witness, the relevance of the witness to the case, the content of the witness's likely testimony, and the type and applicable jurisdiction of the case. Although somewhat counterintuitive, the general rule is that the more cooperative and helpful a witness, the less an investigator should seek to lock him into his account, making a declaration, for example, a more appropriate vehicle to perverse his testimony. Conversely, the less cooperative or more harmful a witness, the more the investigator should lock him into his account, making a verbatim statement more ideal—because the more detail an uncooperative witness provides, the more opportunity there is for possible impeachment during trial. The decision not to lock helpful witnesses into detailed and potentially damaging testimony is critical, since the statements may be discoverable by the opposition. The case type and jurisdiction are also important, since those factors influence whether the documents will be discoverable by the opposition according to the prevailing rules of discovery.

Verbatim statements are taken immediately after the conclusion of an interview, when the witness is still present. Statements may be written by the witness, or dictated by the witness and written by the investigator. The method is generally a matter of personal preference and practicality. For dictated statements, the investigator informs the witness that she wants to write a verbatim account of the events to ensure accuracy, and then asks the witness to reiterate what he said during the interview, starting from the beginning. An investigator should avoid using the word "statement," however, which sounds too legalistic, and she should never explicitly ask a witness whether he will agree to provide a statement. Instead, she should simply state the need to get the facts straight and gently prod the witness to start again from the beginning. The investigator then writes down what the witness says word for word—being sure to skip lines on the notepad to provide space for any corrections—until the witness relays the entire event in one narrative. While it is acceptable to ask the witness questions during this monolog, or to ask him to slow down or clarify a particular area, the statement should reflect the event entirely in the witness's own words. Sometimes, however, an investigator will choose to include questions within the statement, as in the following example:

Q: *What did you do after you saw the gun?*
A: *Well, when I saw the gun I was just, like, scared, you know, and I started running down the street.*

After writing the complete statement, the investigator should add language substantially similar to the below example on the header and footer of the document. Sometimes, investigators use pre-made statement forms that already contain this language. When forms are not used, however, it is best to begin with the statement before writing the header, skipping several lines on the top of the first page to allow enough space for the header after completion of the statement. Although the following language is not required to make a statement useful for purposes of impeachment, the document might not otherwise be admissible without a sworn oath and signature. At the beginning of the statement, write:

This is the statement of [interviewee first and last name], date of birth [mm/dd/yyyy], Social Security number [123-45-6789], address [1234 Anywhere Rd, AnyCity, State, zip], given to [Your name], an investigator working for attorney [Attorney name]. [Attorney name] represents [client name] in [case name] in [court where case is held]. This statement was taken at [location of interview] on [date] at approximately [time].

It is okay if the witness refuses to provide his Social Security number or date of birth. The investigator should simply collect whatever information the witness will provide. At the footer, she should insert the following language:

I have read and have had read to me this [number of pages] page statement [and attached document, diagram, or photograph, if applicable]. I have had an opportunity to make any corrections, deletions, and/or additions to this statement. I solemnly affirm under penalty of perjury that this statement is true, correct, and complete.

After completing a verbatim statement and writing the above language at the header and footer of the statement, the investigator should position the document such that both she and the witness can read it simultaneously. The investigator should then, pointing at every word with the tip of her pen or a similar instrument, read the entire statement to the witness as he reads along silently. She should ask the witness if he can read the handwriting to establish that the witness is literate, and pay special attention to such factors as whether the witness is wearing glasses and whether his eyes are moving in conjunction with the movements of her pen. With every necessary change, the investigator should draw a single line through the verbiage that must be excised—never completely scratching out a word or sentence—and ask the witness to initial the change. Additions should be added by the investigator within the skipped lines. This is the reason why double-spacing is so important. The witness should then initial both before and after any additions. Upon the completion of each page, such that the statement reads exactly what the witness said and he has initialed each deletion or addition, the investigator should ask him to sign and date the page. She should then inconspicuously take that page and place it outside the witness's reach, such as in a briefcase. Otherwise, he may try to take it back. In the event that the witness changes his mind about signing a statement in the middle of the process, the completed pages retained by the investigator may still be useful. The final statement may be significantly marked up with edits and initials, but this is okay, because it shows the statement was given voluntarily, and it proves that the witness had ample opportunity to make changes. The statement is now an ironclad and detailed account of the witness's likely testimony.

For statements written by the witness or typed on the spot, the process is substantially similar, although the investigator necessarily sacrifices some control in the former and spontaneity in the latter. For example, if the witness is tasked with writing his own statement, it may be difficult for the investigator to follow the necessary format or to get him to stay on topic. With typed statements, it may be impractical or awkward to bring a laptop and printer to the field during an interview. Otherwise, the investigator should obtain these statements exactly the same as with statements that she writes herself. It is still necessary to include the legalese, to review the entire completed statement with the witness word for word, and to allow the witness to make corrections.

In contrast to verbatim statements, declarations and affidavits are typically obtained after the conclusion of an interview and after completing the interview report. Because declarations and affidavits are only distinguished by whether they are notarized or not, we will hereafter refer to them collectively as *declarations*. The goal of a declaration is not exclusively for the purposes of impeachment; rather, it is also to preserve helpful testimony in its most pristine form. In some instances, a declaration may even be admissible as stand-alone testimonial evidence, such as to support or oppose a motion for summary judgment in a civil case.

When preparing for follow up meetings with witnesses to obtain declarations, the investigator should write as much of the witness's declaration as possible in advance of the meeting. This will save time and make the process run smoother, allowing the investigator to fill in the blanks and supplement the declaration with new information. She can then anticipate what the witness will say, based upon the earlier interview. While it is ideal to have the same investigator return to obtain the signed declaration, it is not a strict requirement. In the event that a second investigator is conducting the follow-up interview, she will be guided by the information contained in the investigative report and other third-party accounts, such as those of the client or other witnesses. When preparing draft declarations, it is acceptable for the investigator to fill in the gaps with what she expects to be true and what she suspects to be the facts, based upon other evidence gathered during the investigation. In the event that the witness has no firsthand knowledge of the secondhand information in the draft, it can easily be deleted. At this stage, the investigator should draft the declaration in a manner that is ideal from the standpoint of the case's hypothesis, provided that it is consistent with what the witness previously said and with the other known facts of the case.

All declarations and affidavits essentially follow the same format:

My name is [name of signatory or affiant]. I am over eighteen (18) years of age, competent to testify, and I make this affidavit having personal knowledge of the following facts:

1. [Substance in concise language]
2. [Substance in concise language, etc.]

I solemnly affirm under penalty of perjury that the contents of the foregoing paper are true and correct to the best of my knowledge, information, and belief.

For each substantive numbered point, the investigator should sum up the facts of the case in succinct, chronological paragraphs, written in the first person from the standpoint of the witness. The date, exact setting, names of the actors, tone, and scenario should be included with as much detail as possible. She may also attach exhibits referenced in the body of the declaration. If the witness insists on being "fair" to the protagonist, the investigator may add inadmissible and generalized comments so as to give the good with the bad. Consider the following example for a racial discrimination case:

13. Although I thought Mr. Simmons was an excellent manager, he frequently referred to Asian-American employees as "those gooks."

Mr. Simmons may or may not have been a good manager, but he still frequently used a racial slur to refer to his Asian employees. Notice that in the above example, the real word is used for the offensive racial slur, instead of a paraphrase or abbreviation. For declarations, as opposed to verbatim statements, what does not help the case may actually hurt it, so it is important to avoid admissible information that is not supportive of the hypothesis. The investigator should be careful with qualifiers and should not put the witness in a position where he will be impeached by absolutes. As with statements, she should always be sure to include the page number and date on the footer of each page of the document, and the witness should initial and date each page, as well.

It is essential for the investigator to know the law and incorporate it wherever possible, keeping at the forefront what she is trying to prove in the case and how it will be introduced into evidence. Never summarize what someone said when it is important, and employ quotation marks in order to increase the likelihood that the statement will be admissible. She should also draft the declaration with hearsay exceptions in mind. Knowing that one hearsay exception is an excited utterance, consider the below example.

16. *In a fit of excitement Mrs. Jones uttered, "Get your hands off of me!"*

It is always best to conduct interviews at the investigator's office, but because of considerations regarding the witness's convenience, it is sometimes necessary to meet in a public area near the witness's home or work. During this second interview to obtain a declaration, the investigator should bring a laptop computer, a portable, battery-powered printer, and all necessary cables, remembering to have a full charge on all batteries as there may be no power source at the location. It is also important to consider extra paper and extra ink cartridges. Chain restaurants are excellent meeting points for declarations, and restaurant booths are preferred because they generally provide sufficient surface area and privacy. Upon entering the restaurant, the investigator should determine if there are any electrical outlets nearby as she selects a booth. It is okay to buy a witness a simple meal, but never purchase alcohol for a witness, or drink alcohol in the presence of a witness.

As a general rule, during the meeting the investigator should avoid any printed or saved drafts, as they may be discoverable, and losing or destroying them could lead to a spoliation allegation. In other words, she should make all changes digitally and only print the document when it is perfect. Sometimes, however, drafts are unavoidable because witnesses may want to make changes at the last minute. The investigator may not have perfect knowledge, but the witness probably will not know this, so the investigator should talk with confidence and listen carefully to the witness, continually incorporating his answers into the declaration. A witness will often disclose a great deal of information when he thinks the investigator already knows what happened. It is generally acceptable at this stage (since the witness was already interviewed) to tell the witness what other witnesses have said and to ask him to confirm whether he witnessed the same. The investigator must take ample time to proofread the final draft for any grammatical, spelling, or other mistakes, as the declaration is probably discoverable once it is printed and reviewed by the witness. When ready to print, the investigator should read the declaration aloud to the witness and ask him to confirm that it is entirely correct, thereby avoiding drafts and committing him to his story.

If the witness refuses to sign the final declaration, the investigator should never agree to give the witness a draft to sign and return to her at a later date. If the witness won't sign the document at that time, and she does not believe he will sign it, leaving the draft with the witness may cause it to fall into the hands of the opposition. Similarly, the investigator should avoid emailing drafts or final versions to a witness, as the document, drafts, and even metadata will likely end up in the opponent's hands. As with verbatim statements, once the document is signed, the investigator should immediately place it in her briefcase or otherwise out of the witness's reach. If the document is left on the table, the witness may ask for it back.

It is sometimes necessary to obtain declarations from non-local witnesses. When an in-person meeting is not possible, the investigator should determine at the conclusion of the telephone interview if the witness is open to the possibility of signing an affidavit. She should then prepare an interview report and a draft declaration. She should determine the likelihood that the witness will return a signed declaration of his own fruition, based upon the degree of cooperation exhibited by the witness during the interview. It is always better to hire a local investigator to personally deliver the declaration to the witness for signature, and this advice should be relayed to the client. In the event the client does not want to shoulder the extra cost of hiring an outside investigator, she should contact the witness via telephone with the draft affidavit open on her computer screen. She should remind the witness that he previously mentioned he would be open to the possibility of signing an affidavit, and ask him if he has a few minutes to review the draft. If he claims not to have time, reschedule the telephone meeting. The key is to get a time and date scheduled. If he does have a few minutes, review the entire declaration with him from beginning to end and make edits during the call, trying to keep the language in the declaration as similar to the draft as possible. If the investigator decides to hire an outside investigator to deliver the declaration, she should advise the witness that someone will be in touch with him within the next few days to arrange to deliver the document for his signature. If she decides not to hire an investigator, she should ask the witness for his email address and send an email substantially similar to the following example, with the declaration as a .pdf or similar immutable document:

Dear [Witness's name]:

With reference to our conversation a few minutes ago, please find attached the declaration that we produced. Once you have had a chance to review this again, please scan and return this signed document to me via email, or fax a signed copy to me at the fax number below, and then mail the original to my office at the address below. Feel free to make any necessary minor changes, but please give me a call if you need to change any of the substantive language. You can make minor changes by putting a single line through any words that you would like to remove and writing any words that you would like to add in the space between the lines, making sure to initial both the front and back of each alteration. Let me know if you have any questions or need more information. Thanks for your help!

[Name, address, telephone and fax number of investigator]

If an outside investigator needs to be hired, do so now, after the witness has already agreed to the language in the declaration. Simply send a digital copy of the declaration to the investigator with the witness's contact information and clear instructions to obtain the signature. Once the outside investigator has obtained the signed declaration, he will fax and mail a copy to the investigator directly. If she does not receive the faxed affidavit within a few days, she should begin contacting the witness (or the outside investigator, if applicable) to politely remind him to send it to her as soon as possible. She should do the same if she does not receive the mailed original within a few weeks. The declaration should be mailed to the investigator directly, so that she, and not the client, can be responsible for ensuring its completion. Lastly, the investigator should forward the executed declaration to the client as soon as it is received.

Practical Exercise: With at least one other student, conduct a mock interview, where one student is the investigator and the second student is the witness. The investigator will interview the witness about what he did on the Tuesday of the previous week. After the interview, the investigator will take a verbatim state-

ment from the witness about the events of that day, making sure to sign and date every page, and to initial every change. Then reverse roles.

Conclusion

Private investigation is fundamentally the business of selling investigative reports to customers, and gathering and documenting evidence for a fee. Investigations are a waste of time and money if they are not properly documented. For this reason, proper documenting and evidence gathering are essential investigative skills. For example, the formidable skill necessary to conduct a good interview or interrogation is insufficient to solve a problem alone. Without proper documentation, the potential testimonial evidence gleaned during an interview is not actionable and therefore largely useless. An investigator must get into the habit of viewing every action that she undertakes during an investigation—every database inquiry, question, response, and observation—as something that she may have to testify about at some later date. To buttress this possible testimony, she must take copious notes, write reliable and accurate reports, and know when and how to obtain declarations and statements.

Part IV
Types of Investigations

9

Background Investigations

There are two legitimate reasons to conduct a background investigation: due diligence and impeachment. The latter type of investigation involves gathering information for use in impeaching the veracity of witnesses who may testify at any court, board, or committee proceeding. What constitutes an "impeachable" act admissible in court varies by jurisdiction. In Virginia, these acts include prior inconsistent statements and convictions for crimes of moral turpitude within the past ten years. In contrast, a background investigation that is intended for purposes of due diligence[1] is intended to verify the accuracy of information prior to making some meaningful decision. Examples of due diligence investigations include the identification of assets and liabilities for a business entity prior to a merger, or an employer vetting a job candidate prior to offering her a position. The idea is that executives who are tasked with making important decisions affecting other people must exercise a certain amount of diligence, because the cost of possible mistakes far outweighs the menial cost of conducting a thorough background check before a decision is made.

The essential theory behind background checks for purposes of due diligence is that the best predictor of future behavior is past behavior. In the case of employment decisions, this is why companies care about prior criminal convictions, poor credit history, dishonest professional and educational references, a demonstrated lack of job stability, and a pattern of filing unsubstantiated lawsuits against former employers.

All investigations begin by first stating the problem or understanding what needs to be accomplished.[2] In the case of an employment background check, the problem is comprised of four goals: finding a candidate who (1) meets the basic requirements of the position; (2) meets as many of the preferential qualifications of the position as possible; (3) is a good fit for the position; and (4) does not have any factors that disqualify him from the position. Unfortunately, employers performing background investigations often consider only the last goal, ignoring the other aspects of the problem and choosing instead only to search for negative or disqualifying information about a candidate. By remaining ever cognizant of all four goals of the given problem throughout an investigation, and by working methodically towards meeting them all, investigators can be optimally effective in helping clients achieve their goals.

To illustrate this process by a case study, Dinolt Becnel & Wells Investigative Group LLC once conducted in-depth investigations on a pool of approximately three hundred job candidates for an open investigator position located at a client's company. After identifying the problem, most employment decisions begin with reviewing resumes or applications, and at my company this task fell on Michael, an administrative assistant at the firm.[3] We began by establishing a list of basic criteria for the position—these are attributes that, if not met, disqualify a person from the position. For this position, these included a four-year college degree, a minimum one year of fulltime interviewing experience, and demonstrated, strong organizational skills. This step is analogous to forming the hypothesis, because it begins to identify the attributes we were looking for in our investigation. Throughout the various stages of the investigation, we continually returned to those specific attributes that we identified as being necessary to making the correct hiring decision. After initially reviewing three hundred resumes, Michael determined that all but ten did not meet even the basic qualifications for the position. He was able to establish that, of the ten remaining candidates, only two had preferential qualifications. These are qualifications that make a candidate more desirable, but they are not expressly required. Specifically, one candidate, Simon, had experience conducting financial investigations for the National Association of Securities Dealers (NASD, now called the Financial Industry Regulatory Authority or FINRA), and the other, Christian, was bilingual.

As the firm's managing partner, the task fell on me to interview the ten candidates that we identified as qualified for the position. However, when I called to schedule interviews, only six returned my call, including Simon and Christian. As one of many possible investigative tools, conducting interviews is an example of observing and experimenting in order to test the hypothesis that was established at the onset of the investigation. The other four candidates were Richard, William, Julie, and

Jennifer. During my interviews, I determined that William did not meet the basic requirements for the position, because he lied about his qualifications on his resume. I also determined that Christian and Jennifer were probably not good fits for the position; both were not able to adequately articulate why they wanted the job, and I ultimately feared they would each choose to remain at the client's company for a short time and then pursue government jobs. This left three strong candidates, who all met the basic qualifications. One of them had a preferential attribute. For all candidates interviewed, I was required to maintain, for a period of three years, copies of my notes, the applicants' resumes, and all documents that affected our decision to hire or not to hire those individuals.[4] There is no requirement to keep the resumes of applicants who did not meet the basic requirements for the position.

The task of searching for disqualifying factors was performed by Robert, one of my investigators, and me. Importantly, in hiring decisions there are strict limitations regarding what factors one can rely upon. For example, in Virginia, it is only permissible to rely on criminal records if the case ended in a conviction and was not subsequently sealed or expunged. Using civil records is generally only permissible if the records relate in some way to the position. Similarly, employers may only rely on credit reports if the position has a financial component. Just as with the basic requirements, it is imperative that the disqualifying factors be clearly identified at the onset of the investigation. In this case, the factors that would disqualify an applicant from the position included any criminal convictions within the past ten years, any material misstatement on the resume or during the interview, and any significant, negative credit history within the past three years. It was determined that I would contact the applicants' references, while Robert conducted the criminal, civil, credit, and educational institution checks.

Robert began his portion of the background check by first securing a release of information from each of the final three candidates so that he could legally obtain their credit and educational records. It is illegal for an investigator to access a credit report without a release of information, with a few specific exceptions,[5] and most educational institutions will not release school transcripts without the student's written consent. Investigators may obtain credit reports by contacting one of the major credit bureaus or through an intermediate vender. Educational records may be obtained by contacting each institution directly, asking for the student records department, and then faxing the release. Whether a candidate's grades are relevant to the position depends on how long she has been in the workforce after graduation. In this case, Robert used the releases only to obtain the dates of attendance and graduation for each candidate, because this information is useful to verify the accuracy of the resumes.

While waiting for the results of the educational and credit record requests, Robert began conducting the criminal and civil portion of the background check. There is nothing analogous to the National Crime Information Center (NCIC) check in the private sector, except for perhaps Public Access to Court Electronic Records (PACER), which only offers nationwide access to federal court records. The NCIC check is a national criminal information repository operated by the FBI and generally accessible only by law enforcement agencies. It is strictly forbidden and illegal for private investigators to access NCIC, and there are substantial penalties for doing so. Therefore, criminal checks in the private sector are typically conducted by first determining where the subject has lived within the scope of the investigation (e.g., ten years) and then conducting individual searches in those jurisdictions for relevant records. Sometimes private investigators also search records in the jurisdictions that neighbor the areas where the subject lived. There is no more reliable way, other than paying someone to search every courthouse in the country, to conduct a search that will identify every possible record relating to a subject. The same imperfect method is used for conducting both civil and criminal history checks. In our case, Robert first ran an investigative consumer report that contained the address history for each applicant using an investigative database.[6] He then began searching those individual jurisdictions for any records relevant to our investigation.

As a general matter, most criminal and civil court records are open to the public and are physically housed at the courthouses or their storage facilities in those jurisdictions. Each jurisdiction differs markedly in how that information is accessed. Many counties and states now make their records available online in searchable databases. For example, Virginia offers online access to most, but not all of its court records. However, some circuit courts are not accessible online, and district court records in the Commonwealth are routinely destroyed after ten years. Although available online, this information is set up so that the investigator has to search in each jurisdiction individually, which can be very time consuming. It is also possible to conduct a statewide criminal background check in many states, provided the subject has provided consent. In Virginia, for example, the subject must first fill out a form available at any Virginia State Police station, which the investigator then sends to the police, who will conduct the criminal records search. However, since the turnaround time for this process is typically several weeks, such statewide criminal searches have few useful applications, and investigators typically use the online court records option.

Unfortunately, in many other jurisdictions of the country, the investigator must physically search for the records at the local courthouse, sometimes by culling through records stored in large bound books or on microfiche. Luckily, many companies offer onsite record searches in nearly every county in the United States. Therefore, it is relatively easy to search for records on a subject who once resided in Hawaii, for example, even if it is not economically feasible to fly there to conduct the physical search oneself. Often, the mere existence of a court record is not sufficient to determine its relevance to an investigation, so the investigator must obtain copies of the document inside the court jacket. These records are sometimes only obtainable by physically going to the courthouse and requesting copies (or hiring someone to do it for you), although some courts will produce copies via telephone or through the mail.

After Robert completed his portion of the background check, it was determined that Richard, who had several delinquent credit accounts in active collection status, was disqualified, but that Simon and Julie had no records which would disqualify them for the position. Although we identified the disqualifying factors in Richard's credit record, we were still required by law[7] to notify him about our findings in writing and to give him an opportunity to contest our findings. In this case, Richard did not contest the information that we uncovered, and his name was removed from the running.

Meanwhile, before Richard had become disqualified, I began the process of contacting the references at the companies where our three final applicants had worked, and I immediately encountered a red flag with regard to Simon's previous employer. Although he disclosed during his interview that he had been laid off from a position where he worked briefly as an analyst after resigning from NASD, I discovered that he was the only person to be laid off, which I thought was unusual. Additionally, the reference he provided was not his immediate supervisor; rather, it was the director of human resources for the company, who was decidedly tightlipped about Simon's performance and the reasoning behind his termination. Although it is not unusual for companies concerned about possible defamation lawsuits to provide only the employee's title and dates of employment, in this case my suspicion about the layoff made it somewhat troubling. Simon's prior employer also happened to be our client, and I knew several people who worked at the company, so I contacted them directly to see if I could learn more information about the reason Simon was terminated. These individuals agreed to provide information, despite their firm's policy of not providing substantive referrals. I discovered that Simon was probably terminated because he struggled to do the work of an analyst. There was a real question, however, about whether this discovery disqualified him on the basis of not meeting any of the basic requirements of the position. To make this decision, I had to revisit Simon's resume to determine how his previous position compared to the position to which he was applying today.

Also, while interpreting the data, I recognized that I had a conflict of interest that posed a potential ethical dilemma. If I based my decision not to hire Simon on the information provided by my colleagues, who had given me information "off the record" and in violation of their own stated policies, I was potentially exposing my client to a lawsuit. However, ignoring this information would mean that I did not have the best interests of my other client at the forefront of my hiring decision. Recall that any *seeming* conflict of interest is inherently a conflict of interest and must be disclosed. It is important to consider, also, that getting fired from a job does not necessarily make one a risky hire. I decided to wait to make a decision on whether Simon's prior termination demonstrated a lack of pertinent skills until after we completed our investigation.

It turned out that one of Richard's references also described him as having substandard organizational skills. Since this information came directly from his last supervisor I considered it a clear-cut disqualifier; more significant than the derogatory credit records discovered by Robert.

Julie's former employers only had glowing words to say about her, and, coupled with the portion of the check completed by Robert, this made her a very strong candidate. Recall, however, that Simon had a preferential attribute established at the beginning—financial investigative experience—that should have given him an edge over Julie in our decision. Because the information about Simon's termination was discovered informally and its use posed a potential conflict of interest between us and one of our clients, this was a very touchy decision. All of the other factors under consideration were equal.

Discussion: *After drawing conclusions at the end of the above investigation, which candidate should have been hired? Should the conflict of interest have been a contributing factor in the decision? Why or why not? Also, we stated the problem with regard to an employee background investigation as one comprised of four goals. Now, state the problem for a background investigation intended to impeach a witness.*

10

Missing Persons Investigations

Missing person investigations conducted in the private sector normally involve teenage runaways, although sometimes they can involve younger children and occasionally adults. When working for the parents of missing children, it is the unwritten industry standard to discount the cost of the investigation so as not to profit too much from the misery of the family. Missing person investigations of children and teenagers can be very labor intensive, involving exhaustively interviewing friends of the runaway or staking out known hangout locations. Investigative consumer reports obtained from databases, which derive most of their information from the headers of credit applications containing the addresses and other information of applicants, are rarely of direct help in these missing person cases because children and teenagers generally do not have any credit history, and the address information provided by the databases are typically already known by the client.

Because of the costs involved, these investigations are often initiated by making informed guesses about the whereabouts of the missing person by reviewing cell phone records and online networking accounts. Our firm has had success employing a technological approach to optimize our chances of locating runaways with limited funds. For example, by uploading the digital cell phone records of runaways into i2 Analyst's Notebook, a software program that allows an investigator to graphically analyze complicated numerical data, we have been able to identify patterns of behavior exhibited by runaways based on call records that might not have been discernable had we only culled through the phone bills themselves. For example, by realizing that the sum of the duration of calls to a particular number decreased markedly after the disappearance, the investigator may hypothesize that the subsequent calls shortened in duration because the runaway was then spending more time with the individual associated with that telephone number. In this example, the investigator would be well advised to identify the subscriber of that telephone number by using investigative databases and stake out her residence for any sign of the missing teenager.

Social networking sites such as Facebook and Twitter provide great intelligence that is highly useful in locating young, Internet-savvy runaways. Users of these websites routinely post photographs, contemporaneous commentary regarding their social interactions, philosophical musings, and other sometimes valuable information. However, the privacy settings associated with these sites sometimes require the investigator to either access the information through someone who is already an online "friend" of the teenager, or by establishing a false online identity using information known about the teenager's interests, and hoping that she will accept the solicitation of friendship. The latter is the same technique often employed by pedophiles to meet children online, but it works equally well for investigators interested in helping bring teenagers safely home.

It should be mentioned, however, that not all homes actually are safe. Many teenagers run away to escape abusive situations at home. It is the investigator's moral obligation to report any credible evidence of abuse or neglect when working on cases involving minors. I once spoke to a police detective from Miami who said that he hated working runaway cases, because every time he found the wayward teenager, she would invariably say that her father had raped her. In the detective's eyes, if the teenager was telling the truth, then she was better off having left home, but, if the teenager was lying about the sexual assault, than her parents, who would then be under investigation themselves, would have probably been better off had their daughter stayed away. In other words, the scenario that often played out in this detective's runaway cases presented little chance for a happy ending. Unfortunately, this is a common theme in the private sector, as well.

Some missing persons cases do not involve children at all. It is generally perceived as unethical to locate missing adults for private clients unless the investigator—after locating the missing adult—first obtains consent to release his whereabouts to the client. This practice is intended to prevent working for stalkers, the mafia, or other parties possibly interested in using private investigators to contact people they wish to harm in some manner.

To illustrate these difficulties, we were once contacted by the sister of a missing young man who had gone to meet some "friends" and had not returned for two weeks. When we questioned the woman about the people her brother had gone to meet, she confessed that her brother, a drug dealer, had actually gone to buy a large quantity of cocaine from several associates whom she only knew by nickname. We declined to accept the case, instead advising her to go to the police. Two days later the young man's body was found in a burned up van. He had been tortured and executed by a rival drug crew. While there may not have been anything ethically wrong with accepting this case, per se, it illustrates how the underworld of drugs and violence can sometimes cross over into our world, and how it is unwise to accept without question what a prospective client offers as a rationale for wanting to hire us.

It is not always unethical or problematic to accept cases locating missing adults, and it is sometimes necessary to make an exception. One such exception was when my firm was hired by a distraught wife, whose husband, who had an unknown neurological condition, went missing in New Delhi. The husband, John K., was an elderly Maryland resident and an ex-National Security Administration (NSA) official who recently began having frequent psychotic episodes, and doctors in the United States were unable to determine the cause. John did not believe he was sick and was highly resistant to treatment. In a ploy to get John to see a specialist in England, his wife, Molly, first enticed him to travel to India to visit family. However, before John made it to the clinic in England on his return trip, he disappeared at the New Delhi International Airport. Molly, who had only left John alone for a few minutes, was concerned that her husband had forgotten who he was and had become disoriented or lost. She feared he also may have been led astray by one of the thousands of con-artists that frequent New Delhi, or that perhaps he had wandered outside and gotten into an accident.

When Molly called my firm, she was hysterical and very desperate. She had contacted dozens of agencies in India, England, and the United States in an effort to find one that would investigate her husband's disappearance. Each agency told her that they had no jurisdiction to conduct an investigation or that, as an adult, John was free to go wherever he pleased. My first concern was in verifying that John was, in fact, not of his right mind, and, before agreeing to accept the case, I requested that Molly provide me a letter from one of his doctors in the United States, which she did. Satisfied that her story was legitimate and there was a valid reason for an investigation, I had Molly sign a contract for our services and then asked her for a retainer to cover the estimated costs of a preliminary investigation involving lobbying U.S. law enforcement, Interpol, and the New Delhi Police to begin searching for John. I also agreed to coordinate with an Indian investigative firm to help us locate John on the ground in New Delhi, but this was not the central part of my strategy. Having been to New Delhi, I believed there was little chance that we would locate John in that sprawling and chaotic metropolis without the aid of the police.

One thing working to our advantage was that John had several credit cards with him. So, I instructed Molly to set up online accounts for these cards and monitor their activity hourly. This ended up being highly fruitful, because, even before we were officially hired, Molly informed us that it appeared John had taken a plane from New Delhi to Paris. Obviously, this new fact completely upended our understanding of what the investigation was going to entail. In this case, stating the problem was easy: We need to locate John and transport him back to the United States. But given the fact that he was purportedly in a foreign country nearly 3,000 miles away, and that we had limited information—not to mention, a limited budget—we had to carefully form our hypothesis to fit our capabilities.

When we discovered that John was in France, we identified an investigator in that country. The investigator was a member of the Counsel of International Investigators (CII), an international private investigator association, and we retained his services to have him remain in a standby position in Paris while we narrowed down John's whereabouts using online credit card records. We used an investigator from CII, as opposed to hiring an investigator who we found through an Internet search or some other unproven source, because we have learned from experience that CII members are more likely to identify closely with the private investigative profession and adhere to its standards of practice and ethics. As a sound business practice, we engaged the French investigator with a contract that clearly laid out our expectations and the parameters of the investigation.

After we hired the French contract investigator, we waited for other telling credit card transactions to appear on John's statements. While we were waiting for these new clues to register, I called every contact I had in the FBI and the local police authorities in an effort to file a missing persons report that we could provide to the Paris police, who could then issue a lookout bulletin for John. This was part of the initiation of the observation and experimentation phase of the investigation. I tried every argument I could think of to urge them to file a report, including telling the FBI that John's knowledge, gleaned from his former role at the NSA, could present a possible national security issue if it fell into the hands of a foreign government or terrorist organization. Ultimately, however, no agency was willing to get involved or to otherwise help us locate John. Our effort to persuade Interpol, an international police agency based in Lyons, France, to take an interest in the matter was met with similar skepticism and disinterest. It became clear early in the investigation that we were on our own. In interpreting the results of our efforts so far, it seemed that we needed to modify our tactics.

Luckily, after a couple days of waiting, purchases for restaurants and hotel rooms began to appear on John's credit card statements. This provided actionable intelligence that we could use to locate John, possibly even without the aid of any government or quasi-government police agency. The credit card purchases that appeared on John's statements led us to conclude that he was staying exclusively in hotels near the Charles de Gaulle International Airport. Since there were only a handful of potential hotels in the area, we decided the best use of our resources was to send our local investigator with a picture of John to canvass these locations. However, because of personnel shift changes at the various hotels where John was frequenting, it was too time consuming for our contract investigator to talk to more than a few staff members at a time. While some staff members did recall seeing John, nobody was able to provide actionable information that could lead us to John's whereabouts. He was not on the guest registers for any hotel more than once, meaning that he was staying in a different location every night.

Given these difficulties, we ultimately decided to take the drastic step of having Molly cancel John's credit cards. To help mitigate the risk of harm to his health once his funds were cut off, concurrent with cancelling his credit cards we also markedly expanded our search in and around the airport. We instructed our local investigator to pass out fliers with John's picture to every nearby restaurant and shop, the airport infirmary, and the police. So as not to alarm John, should he see one of the fliers and decide to come in voluntarily, we did not include any reference to our firm or the investigation in the flier. Instead, we provided only Molly's name and a local telephone number that we set up to automatically forward calls to her phone as the main point of contact. Within twenty-four hours, John called his wife from the airport, where he had slept the previous night in a waiting area. He reported that he had not eaten in two days and was badly dehydrated, but that he was otherwise okay. I received the call at 3 a.m., and we immediately dispatched our local investigator to meet John at the airport infirmary and to remain with him until one of Molly's relatives could fly from England to bring him back to that country for diagnosis of his underlying neurological condition.

While perhaps not a typical missing persons investigation, John's case illustrates many of the difficulties in finding people who do not wish to be found. It also illustrates how best to utilize whatever resources are available in the given circumstances. For many cases, a trail of bread crumbs in the form of online credit card transactions may not be available, but often phone records, social networking sites, and even human intelligence gleaned from interviews will prove just as useful.

***Discussion:** How many times did the hypothesis change in the investigation involving John? Why do you think the investigative strategy was altered so many times? Assuming that John had gone missing in California, what are some of the associations that might have been used to find competent investigators in that state?*

11

Criminal Investigations

Although the majority of cases worked by private investigators relate to civil matters, including the investigation of accidents and domestic issues, there are two ways in which investigators frequently become involved in criminal matters, too. The first way is when investigators are hired by the victim of a crime, occasionally for an individual citizen, but more often for a company. The second, and more common way, is when investigators are hired on behalf of criminal defendants. In other words, depending on who hired the investigator, she may work on either side of the highly adversarial criminal justice system.

Recall that police do not represent the victims of crime, but rather work on behalf of the citizenry as a whole to prosecute crimes for the good of society. Although the police investigate crimes in an effort to prosecute and incapacitate perpetrators (e.g., via jail or prison), the victim may actually be interested in more than merely incapacitating the criminal, such as restitution for money lost. For example, if a company has been victimized by crime perpetrated by an employee, the company may not want to file criminal charges at all; they may prefer to quietly terminate the employee or seek financial restitution through civil or extrajudicial means. Victims' interests sometimes do not align with the overarching purpose of law enforcement, making it appealing for victims to hire private investigators in lieu of having the police handle the investigation exclusively.

It is rare for private investigators to work on behalf of individual victims of crimes, primarily because most private citizens cannot afford a full-scale investigation and therefore rely on the police to perform their mandate. There are exceptions, however, typically when a victim loses a significant amount of money or when personal emotions are involved.

To illustrate by means of a case study, my firm was once hired by the victim of a hit-and-run accident, a relatively minor criminal offense that does not carry substantial penalties for the defendant and therefore is not a case in which a victim would typically hire a private investigator. In this case, however, immediately after the victim had been broadsided by a car barreling through a red light, he was able to exit his vehicle and take a blurry photograph of the hit-and-run driver, whose hands were shielding his face. The victim took another grainy and largely indecipherable picture of the car's tag as it sped away from the scene. Although any view of the perpetrator's face was obstructed by his hands and the poor quality of the photo, a jailhouse tattoo of a skull was visible on his inside forearm. After three months, the police had not been able to catch the perpetrator, despite the photographic evidence, so the driver hired us to visually enhance the images, run the tags of the suspect's vehicle, and track down the driver. Once we enlarged the image, the tags led me to the suspect's ex-girlfriend, who happily informed me that her then-boyfriend, Herbert J., had admitted wrecking her car after smoking crack on the night of the incident. She also informed me that since the accident he had suffered multiple, non-fatal gunshot wounds during a failed break-in, and he was in jail awaiting felony burglary charges. Herbert was easily identifiable based upon the tattoo in the picture, and he pleaded guilty to the hit-and-run and received a two-month jail sentence, along with the nearly four years he received from the burglary charge.

Although there is a general sense among victims that police are overworked or otherwise not giving their case the attention it disserves, most victims do not seek the services of private investigators due to the high costs involved. Unless there is a strong emotional component that motivates victims to hire a private investigator, they typically leave the matter to the police. However, the motivating emotion can also be as straightforward as a strong attachment to stolen property. One memorable case that my firm worked, for example, involved valuable, heirloom jewelry stolen by an acquaintance.

For another example, consider the case of Chandra Levy, whose family hired private investigators to help solve their daughter's murder in Rock Creek Park in 2001. When investigators hired by the Levy family discovered several bones, including a femur that had been overlooked by the Metropolitan Police Department (MPD) at the crime scene, it drew widespread attention to shortcomings of MPD's Mobile Crime Lab.[8]

It is far more common for private investigators to be hired by companies that sustain an economic loss, because they can more easily shoulder the substantial costs of hiring an investigator. Also, companies are often not interested in pursuing criminal prosecution out of concern for the company's image or because they do not want the distraction of protracted court proceedings. For this reason, understanding the company's motive for initiating the investigation is an important component of stating the problem. An employee may be terminable at will in a given state, and the threshold of evidence required for terminating an employee is far less than the evidence sufficiency required for a criminal conviction (guilt beyond a reasonable doubt), so what the company hopes to achieve alters the parameters of the investigation markedly. Conducting investigations in the workplace also requires a great deal of knowledge about employment law, because employees have many rights that, if violated during the investigation, present a myriad of potential lawsuits against both the employer and the investigator.

On the other side of the criminal equation, it is common for private investigators to conduct investigations on behalf of criminal defendants. Every person charged with a crime in the United States is entitled to representation by an attorney under the Sixth Amendment of the Constitution, and such representation usually has an investigative component. Without an investigator to locate and interview witnesses on behalf of the defendant, it is much more difficult for him to receive a fair trial in the spirit of the Constitution. Because of this basic right, indigent defendants are afforded free representation, although defendants who can afford their own attorneys and investigators are required to pay for this representation themselves. Most jurisdictions in the United States employ attorneys and investigators through public defender agencies, but these agencies are sometimes under-funded and often cannot handle the capacity of criminal cases prosecuted in their jurisdictions. These difficulties are compounded because of conflicts of interest inherent in representing multiple defendants in criminal proceedings in one geographical area. To help with the overflow of indigent defendants, and in cases where the public defender agency has a conflict of interest, attorneys paneled by the court are often appointed to represent defendants who cannot be represented by public defenders. In the federal court system, and in many other jurisdictions, there is a procedure for court appointed attorneys to retain private investigators who are then paid through the court system. In the federal court system, and in Washington, D.C., the procedures for the compensation of investigators are covered under the Criminal Justice Act (CJA).[9] In some jurisdictions, there is a process for investigators to become certified to conduct CJA investigations. In Washington, D.C., for example, investigators are required to complete a course offered at the D.C. Public Defender Service and must submit to a background check conducted by the court.[10] Unfortunately, no analogous program exists in many states (including Virginia) and it is difficult for indigent defendants in these states to obtain investigators, other than in crimes prosecuted in federal court.

For defendants who are able to hire their own defense counsel, the private investigator should be retained by the attorney directly, rather than by the defendant, to ensure she will be covered by legal privilege. In criminal defense cases, the investigator should always insist on being paid a retainer, or at least have the attorney hold the funds in escrow, because, in the event the defendant is convicted, it will be exceedingly difficult to collect money from someone who is in jail. As in all cases, the investigator should have the client sign a contract outlining the scope of the investigation.

These cases invariably follow a defense theory, similar to forming a hypothesis. This theory is largely determined by a careful review of the **discovery**, which is the evidence supplied by the prosecuting attorney, and by what the defendant says actually occurred. What is considered "discoverable," and when it is provided in relation to the trial, varies widely in different jurisdictions. In Virginia, the documentation that the prosecutor is required to provide is typically scant compared to other states, such as Maryland, where the defense is provided essentially all of the government's evidence soon after the charges are filed. This discovery includes police reports, crime scene photographs, and even verbatim, albeit redacted, witness statements.

After carefully reviewing the documents pertaining to the complaint, the first step in defense investigations is to interview the defendant, who may or may not be incarcerated. Because this interview informs the defense theory, it is a critical step. For example, if the defendant states that he was not present at the time the crime was committed, then the case hypothesis may be that he was misidentified by the witnesses who placed him at the scene. Such a theory might be buttressed by an alibi. This theory is most common when the government lacks real evidence, or when the direct evidence[11] is contingent upon a questionable identification. For violent crimes when the identification is strong or uncontestable, it is more common for the hypotheses to focus on the victim's role in the event, such as self-defense or consent (e.g., in the case of sexual assaults) theories. In cases where the government's evidence is strong, or when the evidence supports such a defense, the theory may hinge instead on an insanity defense or on a procedural basis for the exclusion of inculpatory evidence, such as a confession under duress or lack of probable cause for a search.

The conduction of defense investigations mimics other types of investigations with regard to the observation and experimentation phase of the case. For example, in establishing an alibi, the investigator will interview and obtain statements from witnesses who support the alibi, or she will obtain surveillance footage, receipts, and other evidence from the places where the defendant may have been at the time the crime was committed. With regard to identification, it is important to keep in mind that witnesses' memories are notoriously subject to suggestion. For example, a witness who is shown the same photograph in two different photo arrays will often subconsciously come to associate the photograph with the crime, thereby "positively" identifying the suspect the second time.[12] Therefore, to investigate a misidentification, the investigator will question a witness about the circumstances under which he was shown a photo array or asked to identify the suspect at a line up, to ascertain whether the methods used by the police tainted the process. The investigator must, while interviewing the witness, pay careful attention to the way in which the witness describes the suspect. Even slight discrepancies in details, such as whether the suspect was wearing a red hat or a brown hat, can call into question the underlying identification. With regard to self-defense and other theories, the investigator will question witnesses to the crime, delving into the exact details of the event that might not be apparent from the government's discovery: the who, what, where, when, why, and how of the investigation. It is also important to investigate the circumstances of the crime by examining, photographing, and diagramming the physical crime scene, and conducting thorough background checks of the victim and all witnesses. This allows the investigator to possibly discover factual inconsistencies with a government witness's account, or to document a propensity toward violence or dishonesty.

Our firm was once hired by the family of a college student, David, in Richmond, Virginia, after he was charged with felony sexual assault as part of an alleged gang rape at a party near the university. The female victim, Michelle, who was nineteen years old and also a college student, resided in North Carolina and had been visiting her friend, Stacy, at the university over spring break when the incident occurred. Stacy was friends with David, and they invited Michelle to attend a party consisting of dozens of mutual friends at a house that David rented with a friend, who was then out of town. Several days after the party, Michelle contacted the police to report that she had been raped by four men at the party. The only name she was able to provide was David's, and he was promptly arrested and interrogated; although he refused to provide information to the police, or to provide the names of anyone who attended the party. His family hired a criminal attorney, who hired our firm to conduct a thorough investigation of the case.

The case was assigned to our associate investigator, Janet, who promptly traveled to Richmond to meet with David. He told her that he had, in fact, had sex with Michelle, as had several of his friends at the party, but that it had been consensual. He said that part of the encounter had been captured on a participant's mobile phone video camera, and that Michelle had joked about the incident with Stacy the next morning. Based on this information, Janet determined the defense theory was that the complainant had consented to have sex with David and the others, and Janet began to test her hypothesis. She first visited David's apartment to diagram and photograph where the alleged assault occurred, so as to orient herself with the location when later talking to witnesses, and to preserve any evidence that may have still been present. While at the crime scene, Janet took dozens of photographs in a coordinated series and created a detailed sketch of the apartment. While examining the bedroom, she found a discarded condom wrapper behind the bed. Ever conscious of the theory of transfer, she took photographs of this piece of evidence, measured its exact location using the rectangular coordinate method, and then used a piece of paper to collect the wrapper and place it in a plastic baggie, which she sealed with tape and initialed. The condom wrapper may not have been related to the alleged assault, but she would not know this until later in the investigation.

When conducting any investigation, it is standard to begin by interviewing the subjects who will likely be the most cooperative and have the most general knowledge about the underlying facts of the case. Those deemed least likely to cooperate, and who have highly specific knowledge about the events in question, are the last to be interviewed. This is because general information supplied by the cooperative witnesses can better prepare the investigator to extract specific information from the less cooperative witnesses. Janet began by interviewing the other party-goers to question them about what they had witnessed. Then she interviewed Stacy, who was deemed to be cooperative due to her friendship with David. Next, she interviewed the thereto-fore unnamed suspects who also had sex with Michelle, and only then did she directly interview the alleged victim herself.

Janet's interviews of the party-goers described a night of heavy drinking and loud music, with Michelle, whom none of them had previously met, appearing both vivacious and intoxicated. She appeared to fit in well with her new friends, they said, and appeared to be somewhat uninhibited in her behavior. According to the police report Janet obtained from the police department, the assault occurred between approximately 2 a.m. and 4 a.m. Unfortunately, nobody at the party, aside from the four suspects, reportedly stayed late enough to witness the events leading up to the alleged assault, so Janet was unable to learn specific information from these witnesses—aside from the fact that the alleged victim had a lot to drink and appeared to be having a good time earlier in the evening. The next step was to interview Stacy, who had left the party around midnight, and the information that she provided to Janet proved to be very telling. Stacy told the investigator that Michelle had come to her apartment and joked that she had been "Eiffel towered" after the party by David and some of his friends. Stacy explained to Janet that being Eiffel towered was a colloquialism for when a woman has sex with one man while performing fellatio on another; the two men clasp hands over the woman's body to form a pose that looks something like the Eiffel Tower. According to Stacy, Michelle made the comment in a lighthearted manner, which indicated that the sex had been consensual. Because this was a Virginia criminal case and statements taken from defense witnesses would not be discoverable by the prosecution, Janet took a verbatim statement from Stacy relaying the conversation that she had with Michelle the morning after the alleged assault. Janet had her sign each page of the statement, locking her into her account of what happened, in case she ever changed her story. Had this been a federal case, Janet would not have taken a statement from Stacy, because it would have been discoverable under the federal rules of evidence. Interestingly, the police never interviewed Stacy, suggesting that Michelle had not provided Stacy's name to the police.

Stacy also told Janet that she was friends with Michelle on Facebook, and that Michelle and others had posted comments about the incident on the site. With this knowledge, Janet, with Stacy's expressed consent, immediately logged onto the website using Stacy's password and reviewed the relevant comments. This was an urgent task, because users can delete comments, making them difficult, although not impossible, to retrieve. It became immediately clear that some people had made disparaging comments to, and about, Michelle regarding what had transpired the night of the incident. For example, one person had written the day after the incident, "lmao! sorry i missed the gangbang last nite! [sic]." Another person had referred to Michelle as a "slut." These and similar comments were significant because they explained why Michelle had a reason to lie about the rape incident nearly three days after it occurred: She was possibly embarrassed about being labeled a slut. Furthermore, in reviewing the history on Michelle's Facebook "wall," Janet discovered that she made frequent references to binge drinking and drug use. She printed out these pages as evidence and obtained a subpoena to serve to Facebook for the login names and IP addresses of the people who had posted the relevant comments.

Janet then set about interviewing the other students who reportedly had sex with Michelle the night of the incident. Two of them refused to cooperate, concerned about being charged in the case. Still, one of the suspects, Jason, a close friend of David, was unperturbed by the prospect of being named in the case and agreed to show Janet a video he had taken on his phone the night of the incident. The video, only about a minute long, was taken from the bedroom doorway and showed Michelle in flagrant delicto, apparently unaware that she was being videotaped with David and one of the others in the so-called "Eiffel tower" position. Janet promptly downloaded this video and preserved it as evidence.

Next, Janet interpreted the results of the investigation, and, with the evidence obtained from the interviews, video, and Facebook comments, she was ready to interview Michelle. Interviewing complainants should always be conducted in person with no advance warning that the investigator is coming. This makes it more difficult for the complainant to back out of the interview. Luckily, because North Carolina has a reciprocity agreement with Virginia, this was not a problem, and Janet flew to Raleigh to make contact with the alleged victim. With no small amount of skill based upon several years of experience conducting investigative interviews, Janet was able to persuade Michelle to be interviewed at a coffee shop in downtown Raleigh. Ultimately, Michelle steadfastly maintained that she had been raped by David and the others, although she claimed that she blacked out during most of the assault and therefore could not remember many of the details. Janet did not disclose to Michelle either the conversation she had with Stacy or the video obtained from Jason. Instead, Janet took a verbatim statement from Michelle detailing all of the facts as she alleged them.

After conducting all the interviews and securing the available evidence, including a sworn statement from the alleged victim, the case was well prepared for trial.

Discussion: What if the complainant lived in Pennsylvania? What would the investigator have to do in order to interview her? Assume that Michelle had hired a private investigator to identify the other men who assaulted her. Would the investigator have ordered the interviews differently? How would the hypothesis have been different?

12

Undercover Investigations

An undercover investigation is not so much a *type* of investigation, as much as it is a tool for obtaining information during an investigation that may be impossible to get via other means. These investigations are sometimes referred to as **overt surveillance**, because the investigator is observing behavior while not attempting to conceal her whereabouts; rather, she is using a cover or pretext to blend into the situation. The term "pretexting" has been in the investigative vernacular for many years, but became something of a dirty word when Hewlett-Packard (HP) executives hired private investigators to investigate a media leak among their board of directors.[13] The investigators used a contractor to contact a telephone company, pretending to be the board member suspected of the leak, and were able to access telephone records that proved he was responsible for the leak. When the investigator's tactics became public, it started a firestorm of public outcry and led to a congressional investigation. Ultimately, the investigators were criminally prosecuted and a new federal law was passed that explicitly banned the pretexting of "confidential telephone information."[14]

Despite fallout from the HP investigation, undercover investigations are still a legitimate and entirely legal investigative method, except in certain specifically defined instances. For example, it is never proper for a private investigator to impersonate a police officer[15] or to pretend to be a doctor, counselor, attorney, clergy member, or any type of government agent in order to obtain confidential information.[16] It is likewise explicitly prohibited to pretext for telephone call records[17] or financial records.[18] Also, ethical rules for attorneys prohibit them from personally engaging in deception or instructing their agents to engage in deception. This means that undercover investigations are not appropriate vehicles to gather information when working for an attorney during active litigation. These rules also apply to state and federal prosecutors, which is why undercover investigations conducted by law enforcement, such as undercover drug purchases, occur before prosecutors become involved in the case.

Undercover investigations can be as simple as calling a client's former employer for a reference check in furtherance of an investigation into defamation, or as complicated as posing as a member of an organization for a prolonged period of time to uncover a conspiracy among its members. During undercover investigations, an investigator must be careful to avoid entrapment, which is the act of suggesting or leading a subject into engaging in illegal or unethical behavior that he otherwise would not have done. What constitutes entrapment is very often just on the other side of a fine line, but the general rule is that it's okay for the investigator to solicit someone to commit a crime, but she may not suggest or otherwise encourage him to commit the crime. It is, however, permissible to set the stage for the illegal behavior by asking questions to illicit conduct that would have likely happened anyway. For example, it would not be entrapment to ask a subject if he has any marijuana to sell—but it would clearly be entrapment if she asked the subject if he wanted to drive with her to a high-drug area so that they could purchase drugs together. In the first instance, if the subject sold marijuana to the undercover operative, then it is reasonable to assume that he probably would have sold the drugs to someone else, whereas in the latter example the subject may not have purchased drugs had the investigator not made the suggestion and offered to drive. In other words, the investigator must allow the subject to incriminate himself.

The key to undercover investigations is for the operative to appropriately blend into her undercover identity, which involves knowing the necessary lingo and having the proper credentials. In cases where an investigator must infiltrate a company, for example, her resume and experience must be consistent with someone who would really be working in that position. An undercover investigator must always appear confident in her identity and be able to think quickly on her feet. My firm was once hired by a nonprofit organization that studied human trafficking and educated governments on ways to prevent it. The organization was based in the United States and had conducted investigations throughout the world, primarily by interviewing sex workers on camera about their origins and how they got to be where they are. The organization hired us to help conduct a similar study of foreign-born prostitutes in Washington, D.C.

Stating the problem of the investigation required an understanding of the dynamics of human trafficking. Many of the women and children that were interviewed had been kidnapped and sold into sexual slavery, or had been tricked into selling their lives away by promises of emigration to a more prosperous place. Another feature of human trafficking, as it relates to prostitution, is there is invariably a pimp—in Asian establishments called the mamasan—who keeps an eye on the women, who are moved around the country periodically to prevent them from making significant connections in any particular city. Interviewing the women required us to first get access through their pimps, and our hypothesis was that we could only identify and interview victims of human trafficking by playing the role of johns. Also working on the case was a staff investigator, Joe, from the client-organization, and a professional cameraman who remained in the vehicle and filmed the outside of the massage parlors and motels where Joe and I would meet the women. We identified the various locations through newspaper ads for Asian massage parlors, and from Internet personal ads offering sex for sale from women with Hispanic-sounding names. The latter sites required us to first call a phone number and speak to the pimp about the meeting location, which was invariably a local motel.

We started the observation and experimentation phase of the investigation by visiting the massage parlors, of which there were about a dozen in the Washington, D.C. area. Because Maryland prohibits the surreptitious audio recording of subjects without their expressed consent, we limited our investigation to establishments in D.C. and Virginia. Joe and I wore hidden, wireless cameras and microphones that broadcast a signal to equipment maintained by the cameraman in the nearby vehicle. I wore a pair of eyeglasses that had a pinhole camera positioned between my eyes. Since the black-rimmed glasses were a bit chunky (think Elvis Costello), we were concerned they would not be effective in a setting as confined as a massage parlor. Still, since the angle and quality of the camera was excellent, we decided to try them out anyway. Joe wore a camera on the strap of his backpack.

Because Joe had more experience than me in this particular type of investigation, it was decided that I would distract the mamasan while he interviewed the prostitutes. In the first massage parlor, a Caucasian doorman checked our ID cards and immediately squinted toward the pinhole camera in my eyeglasses. I stand six-feet, four-inches tall and then weighed a muscular 185 pounds, but this doorman was much bigger, and it was clear that he was onto us from the start.

"Is that a camera in your glasses?" he asked, reaching for my eyeglasses. I stepped out of his reach and laughed, telling him that I did not know what he was talking about. "Yes, it is!" he declared.

My main concern at that point was that he was going to punch me in the face. With that camera perched between my eyes, I would have likely spent the night in the emergency room. In any case, it was clear that we were not going to be getting into this massage parlor, so Joe and I quickly retreated.

"Come on," Joe said to me, pulling me toward the exit, "We don't need this!" By thinking quickly and working together, Joe and I were able to safely extricate ourselves from a volatile situation and continue with our investigation.

Of course, we decided not to continue with the eyeglass camera, and opted for a camera attached to a backpack, similar to the one that Joe was using, instead. Our visits to the subsequent massage parlors were much more fruitful. The typical interaction was for the mamasan to have us each enter a room with a single bed, and then parade before us a group of Asian women wearing colorful patent leather bikinis. The workers appeared to be in their late teens or early twenties, while the mamasan, usually a retired sex worker herself, was typically in her thirties or forties. There was a flat fee for the "massage," but it was made clear in each instance that whatever happened inside the room was between the customer and the girl. In other words, sexual services were paid directly to the worker so that the mamasan could feign ignorance that the parlor was really a front for prostitution, despite the fact that many of the rooms contained hidden cameras allowing the mamasan to watch the activity from another room. In these locations, Joe and I would pretend that only he wanted a "massage," while I made small talk with the mamasan in order to distract her.

At one location, I sat in a room that doubled as both a kitchen and the mamasan's bedroom. We sat on the bed as Joe interviewed one of the girls in another bedroom. Behind the mamasan was a security monitor where I could see Joe sitting on the bed with the girl. To distract the mamasan from looking at the monitor behind her, and to learn information that might be useful for our investigation, I asked the mamasan about her job and where she and the other girls were from—all while she steadily rubbed my clothed thigh! Because of the small size of the room, I had not been able to place the backpack in a location to record my undercover interview. Instead, I set the backpack on the bed opposite from where she was sitting and twisted the strap at an upward angle so her face would be visible while we talked. This only left me with one hand to prevent the mamasan's hand from traveling too far up my thigh! My manipulation of the backpack strap must have appeared to her as a manifestation of nervousness, because she continually assured me that everything would be okay.

Altogether, I was able to prevent the mamasan from turning around to view the monitor and possibly becoming suspicious that Joe and the girl were still fully dressed and not engaging in a massage. I also learned that the mamasan and the other girls were from South Korea, and that she had been in the United States for eight years. She said that she moved between dozens of different cities as her employer dictated, but she had been in D.C. for several months and hoped to stay longer. She told me how the girls would stay in a city for a few months before being transferred to a different city. She became evasive when I asked questions about the terms of their employment or who exactly owned the massage parlor.

After interpreting the data, it was clear that this massage parlor was only one in a network of connected brothels around the country, and the women had very little input about where they worked. Joe discovered during his interviews that the women were required to work six, and sometimes even seven days per week to work off "debts" incurred while they were being smuggled into the United States. My interviews with the various pimps and Joe's interviews with the prostitutes were used in a video to lobby the U.S. government to educate the public about the true nature of massage parlors and escort services.[19] Before the conclusion of our investigation, many people, including some heads of law enforcement agencies, presumed these were victimless crimes, when, in fact, it was (and is) tantamount to sexual slavery, sometimes occurring within blocks of the White House. The D.C. government took notice, and shortly afterward there were raids on many of the massage parlors that we investigated. However, most of the businesses that were shut down simply sprang up in different locations, proving the resilience of criminal enterprises to flourish and continue to operate under the radar.

Practical Exercise: This investigation involved massage parlors, but an undercover investigation might occur in any setting. Using a pretext that does not violate the law, strike up a conversation with a stranger at a shopping mall or other public location and obtain as much personal information about the stranger as possible.

13

Fraud and Financial Investigations

Fraud occurs when someone deceives another person about a material fact that causes the victim some manner of monetary or other harm. It may be prosecuted criminally or civilly in the United States. The individual making the false representation must have known that his statement was false, but this may include offering an opinion as fact, or offering an opinion when there is no reasonable basis to believe that the representation is true. Financial investigations include fraud investigations, but they also span any type of investigation involving monetary loss, including theft and embezzlement. The main distinction between fraud and other types of financial investigations is that fraud does not involve physically taking something, per se, as much as it involves deceit. Consider a case of financial statement fraud in which the executives of a publicly traded company manipulate the company's financial figures to increase the appearance of assets or decrease the appearance of liabilities, thereby deceiving investors, creditors, and regulators. While the executives certainly benefit from this fraud, usually by receiving stock options or bonuses tied to the company's performance, this does not constitute "stealing" in the same manner as, for example, one might steal from a cash register.

Investigators become involved in financial and fraud investigations in several ways. Typically, investigators are hired by companies to investigate theft and fraud perpetrated by their employees, venders, or customers. In these cases, the company has usually already determined that a crime has occurred, but they need an investigator to help identify who was responsible. For example, my firm was once hired by a hospital that was under investigation by the Department of Justice (DOJ) for

Medicare and Medicaid fraud, after billing irregularities were discovered during an external audit. One employee was subsequently indicted and terminated for the fraud, but the hospital decided to be proactive in determining if any other employees had also been involved. I spent several days at the hospital interviewing employees about their knowledge of fraudulent invoices and the underlying billing practices. My investigation ultimately determined that the fraud was probably only perpetrated by the one employee. As in this case, auditors typically identify fraud that spurs the internal investigation, but then outside investigative firms are called in to interview witnesses, gather evidence and the like. Investigating fraud often requires a great deal of knowledge about the industry where the alleged fraud occurred and a thorough understanding of accounting methods; both of which are beyond the scope of this textbook.

Fraud investigations also include external fraud and whistleblower cases. In the latter category, several federal and state laws provide legal protection for employees who blow the whistle on fraudulent activity conducted by their employers. For example, the Sarbanes-Oxley Act of 2002 (SOX)[20] provides protection for whistleblowers at publicly traded companies, and the **qui tam provision** of the False Claims Act[21] allows employees of government contractors that commit fraud to sue their employers on behalf of the government. There are also state whistleblower laws. For example, Bowman claims protect whistleblowers in Virginia companies that violated state and federal criminal laws.[22] With the exception of some claims under qui tam, which roughly translates to, "He who sues for the king as well as himself," most whistleblower investigations focus on the action of alleged retaliation, not on the fraud itself. Because whistleblowers filing SOX or Bowman claims are required to complain about fraud on a basis of good faith, investigators must also examine the underlying criminal allegations to determine if the fraud actually occurred, or at least confirm that the whistleblower reasonably believed that it did. Qui tam, however, is a very unique legal principle in that it allows employees to sue their companies for fraud and to claim monetary damages on behalf of the government, even in the absence of retaliation by the company. The law's intent is to provide an incentive for employees of government contractors to blow the whistle on false claims made to the government. The law also applies to government employees who blow the whistle on contract fraud when agents of the government are also involved in the fraud. My firm has investigated hundreds of qui tam claims, many involving contractors who sold shoddy military equipment to the government during the wars in Iraq and Afghanistan. Upon completion of a qui tam investigation, the case is filed under seal in the appropriate federal court and served to the DOJ, who then conducts its own investigation. The DOJ then either agrees to prosecute the case or declines. If they decline to prosecute, the plaintiff still has the option to prosecute the case with his own private attorney.

External fraud investigations can involve something as simple as a dispute over a misrepresentation in a contract, or they can involve investigations of extensive fraud conspiracies, such as the financial statement fraud perpetrated by Enron, or Ponzi schemes like the con perpetrated by Bernard Madoff.[23] **Ponzi schemes** masquerade as legitimate investments, take in new investors' money, and pay it to earlier investors, essentially redistributing the company's capital instead of legitimate income. In the private sector, such investigations are typically led by disgruntled investors pooled together in class action lawsuits, attempting to recoup some of their losses after the implosion caused by the fraud. Other types of external fraud investigations may be initiated by parties not directly related to the fraudulent transactions. For example, my firm has conducted dozens of major fraud investigations for financial institutions concerned with the misuse of their trademarks in the perpetration of fraud against third-party consumers. In these cases, consumers were scammed after viewing advertisements that purported to come from legitimate money lenders. The advertisements came through different mediums, including telephone, email, and regular mail. Some of the scams employed phony websites that appeared to be those of the legitimate lender, a method of cyber-fraud known as "phishing." Regardless of the method of fraud, consumers are typically tricked into wiring money to the criminals, usually under the guise of an advanced fee, such as for "loan insurance," or some other type of processing fee. In these cases, although the financial institution's actual clients have not lost any money directly, the financial institution is still concerned about the misuse of their company trademark. In other words, it was deemed that when criminals commit fraud with their company's name, it is bad for business.

One such case was an advanced fee scam that involved phishing consumers via a website purporting to belong to the "Aristotle Bank." The consumers were led to apply for loans online and were subsequently called by a toll-free number and told that, because they did not have good credit, they needed to pay an insurance fee totaling anywhere from three to eight percent of the loan value before the loan could be processed. For consumers with poor credit, this can be an attractive offer, as it means they can get a loan with a low interest rate for a relatively small fee. They were told the money needed to be wired to Canada, where the insurance was "cheaper." This type of scam is commonly known as an **advanced fee scam**. Of course, after the customers wired the money, they never received their loan, and eventually the toll-free number and the website were shut down, leaving the victims very little recourse but to call the real Aristotle Bank to complain that they had been scammed. The monetary losses of these victims ranged from about $400 to $2,500.

The problem with investigating advanced fee scams is they often originate in other countries, usually Canada or Nigeria. Because the economic losses are relatively low, the FBI and other federal law enforcement agencies in the United States generally will not investigate them. Meanwhile, the foreign authorities are similarly not concerned about the scams, because none of the victims are citizens of their countries. To be fair, the Royal Canadian Mounted Police operate a task force, known as Phone Busters, formed to target international fraud originating in Canada, but this agency steadfastly refuses to cooperate with private investigators in the United States. Compounding these problems, the perpetrators of these scams are highly skilled at avoiding detection. They often use multiple prepaid mobile phones to route calls through a web of false identities and employ stolen credit cards to pay for any service that could lead an investigator to their identifies. Therefore, in this case, stating the problem involved an acknowledgement that, without the aid of law enforcement, there was very little that could be done from a criminal prosecutorial standpoint about this fraud, assuming that we were able to identify those responsible. Likewise, prosecuting the fraudsters civilly was not likely to be fruitful either, as there were the obvious jurisdictional issues to consider—not to mention the fact that the scammers would likely not respond to a civil summons even if we were able to locate and serve them. We determined the best method to solve this case was to provide leads to local law enforcement agencies where the victims resided in hopes that one of the police departments would solicit the assistance of Phone Busters directly.

We began the investigation by conducting Internet research regarding the phone number and website associated with the scam. By using investigative databases, we were able to identify a name and address associated with the toll-free number—although we assumed this information was probably a false lead. The address was a beauty supply store near Toronto. For good measure, we hired a Canadian investigator to conduct surveillance on the location to determine if there was any suspicious activity occurring. Our hypothesis was that this was a well-organized fraud ring whose members were not careless enough to use their real names and addresses. This case would probably not be solved by running a simple database query. We also believed that the fraudsters were not limiting their fraud to one financial institution. We divided the task of interviewing all the victims, who described the manner by which they were conned in embarrassing detail. They came from all over the United States, from California to Maine. Interviewing the victims provided highly useful information about the number of participants in the scam, their accents, and methods. We knew there was at least one man and one woman, and their accents were described as either Hispanic or South Asian. Hypothesizing that it was a husband-and-wife team perpetrating the fraud, and that their accents were something of a cross between Spanish and South Asian, we thought they might have originated in Guyana, a South American country with a large Indian population. This hypothesis was supported by the fact that the beauty supply store was close to a section of Toronto that was highly populated with Guyanese immigrants.

While the surveillance was ongoing, we also conducted research via online chat groups related to advanced fee scams. We were able to discern that the fraud under investigation appeared to be related to other ongoing scams. These scams were infringing on the trademarks of several other well-known financial institutions. Because I knew a senior corporate security person at one of the other targeted financial institutions, I was tasked with contacting that institution to see if they were investigating the related advanced fee scam. As it turned out, they were, and my colleague agreed to provide us with information related to their investigation if we provided information in return. After checking with our client, we thereafter formed a loose, working partnership with this second financial institution and shared information as it became available. I also contacted each of the assigned police detectives of the local jurisdictions where the victims resided, introducing myself and my firm, and offering information regarding what we had learned about the fraudsters. In each instance, the detectives were glad to receive our information, and they provided us with information gleaned from their investigations as well. Not surprisingly, we had a lot more information to give than they had to offer.

After the surveillance of the beauty supply store did not turn up anything suspicious, we decided it would be helpful to know the other phone numbers called by the original toll-free number. These call details, we assumed, would provide the identities of other victims and demonstrate how the scam was interconnected with other scams. We also thought there was a good chance that call records would provide legitimate leads regarding the whereabouts of the scammers. Because this information is protected by the Telephone Privacy Act and we did not have a subpoena,[24] the only way to retrieve the call records was by contacting the telephone company and asking them directly for the information. The telephone company that owned the toll-free number was very small, so it was not difficult for us to get the owner on the telephone. Once we told him about our case, the owner agreed to provide us with the information needed for our investigation if we agreed to do something for him. The telephone company had a few debtors who collectively owed thousands of dollars, according to the owner, and he wanted us to locate them. If we would do his investigation free of charge, he would give us the telephone records. We agreed, and after conducting the research requested by the telephone company—which we billed to Aristotle Bank as a business expense—we received the records, which showed that the fraud touched nearly every state in the United States. We imported this data into i2 Analyst's Notebook for easier interpretation. When we cross-referenced the phone numbers with information obtained through online chats it was clear that the fraudsters were using the names of several well-known financial institutions. The phone numbers also provided leads to buildings and suspects in and around Toronto.

In light of the fruits of our investigation, it was determined that, short of sending our own investigators to Toronto to personally conduct interviews, there was not much else we could do except to provide all the information we had amassed to the local law enforcement agents. Also, spurred by information provided by my colleague at the other financial institution, we drew a further conclusion. He told me that he had been contacted by a U.S. Secret Service agent involved in a taskforce that had recently began investigating similar scams originating in Canada. Since our case was much more extensive than we expected, we decided that the local police departments probably did not have the resources to properly handle it, and we opted to send our information to the Secret Service task force instead. We do not know what happened to the perpetrators of this scam or the leads that we provided to law enforcement. What is clear, however, is that advanced fee scams originating internationally continue to routinely target American consumers. Aside from the occasional federal task force, virtually nobody in the United States is seriously investigating these crimes, aside from a few financial institutions and their private investigators.

> **Discussion:** *List the tactics employed in the observation and experimentation phase of the advanced fee scam investigation. In your view, was it ethical for the investigative firm to barter with the telephone company's owner to obtain information in return for unrelated investigative services, and then bill those services to another client? Why or why not? How would an investigation into a SOX or Bowman claim differ from a normal fraud investigation?*

14

Insurance Investigations

Aside from law firms, insurance companies hire private investigators more than any other group. The reason for this is obvious: Insurance fraud is extremely common. Even some otherwise honest people believe that scamming insurance companies is morally acceptable—a supposedly victimless crime. From the insurance company's standpoint, however, insurance fraud is not only wrong, it is exceedingly expensive. In fact, insurance fraud is the second most common type of fraud after tax evasion.[25] An insurance investigation is always spurred by an insurance claim filed by the policy holder, sometimes after the initiation of a claim or lawsuit by the person who claims to have been harmed in some manner. There are countless types of insurance claims, from those involving relatively simple medical claims to those involving accidents and willful negligence on the part of the policy holder. In fact, it is possible to obtain an insurance policy for potentially anything that can go wrong in life, from acts of terrorism, to catching a cold and missing work. Insurance is essentially a contract between the insurance carrier and the insured, whereby the insurer agrees to cover the costs in the event of a claim covered by the contract in return for a fee, called the premium, and sometimes a deductible. Insurance companies make money by recognizing the statistical likelihood that an event will occur within a particular demographic. Insurance fraud is costly to insurance companies and consumers because it skews the algorithms insurers use to calculate risk, thereby driving up insurance premiums.

Anything that is not covered on an insurance policy is termed an exclusion. When an insurance company receives a claim, they conduct a degree of due diligence on the claim and the claimant to make sure everything appears legitimate. If there were physical damages related to the claim, as in an automobile accident claim, then a claims adjuster is typically dispatched to survey the damages and help facilitate an estimate. In the event that something does not seem right, the insurance company will conduct an investigation. Sometimes companies investigate all their claims or a sample of their claims as a matter of policy. Many insurance companies have their own internal investigators to conduct insurance fraud investigations—sometimes called special investigation units (SIUs)—but most companies outsource at least part of their investigations. This is a sizable percentage of the work performed by private investigators in the United States.

A common type of insurance case is a **worker's compensation investigation**. This type of investigation is initiated by an insurer to determine if a worker who claimed to be injured at work is faking or exaggerating his injuries. When a worker is injured at work he sees a doctor who recommends medical limitations or restrictions, essentially physical activities the worker should not do because of the injury. To the extent that restrictions prevent the worker from performing his job, he then applies for worker's comp and his employer files a worker's comp claim to the insurance company, which then pays the worker's medical bills and lost wages. The medical restrictions might be that a worker is not permitted to lift more than twenty-five pounds, or that he not remain in a standing position for more than one hour at a time. These investigations typically involve surveillance, although they can also involve interviews and undercover work. Proof of fraud is directly related to the worker's medical restrictions, and the investigator, for example, attempts to videotape everything the worker does in his daily life, ultimately looking for violations of the restrictions. Another way to investigate a worker's comp claim is to directly investigate the alleged accident by interviewing co-workers who witnessed the event, and even non-employee associates of the worker to determine if the injuries were sustained in an accident unrelated to the job. The investigator may sometimes determine that the alleged accident was staged or did not otherwise happen as claimed.

Other types of insurance cases involve premise and product liability claims. A **premise liability claim** occurs when someone is allegedly injured on an insured property. One case investigated by our firm involved a woman who claimed that part of her apartment ceiling fell on her head while she was eating dinner on her couch. She claimed debilitating neck injuries that prevented her from running or lifting more than fifteen pounds. She also claimed that her injuries required her to wear a neck brace and to use a walking cane. Because it was determined that the woman had made several suspicious insurance claims in the past, the insurance company hired us to investigate both the legitimacy of the woman's injuries and the ceiling damage itself. For the latter task, we hired a contractor with a clean record to survey the damage to the ceiling. By determining that the section of the drywall that fell was only two feet in diameter, we learned that the weight of the ceiling, even if wet, could not have caused the claimed neck injuries. To investigate the injuries more directly, our firm conducted periodic surveillance of the woman over several weeks. The surveillance conducted by our investigator captured her on video running to catch a bus, carrying her toddler, and walking unfettered throughout the city, all sans neck brace and cane. The insurance company opted to reject the claim, and the woman thereafter dropped her lawsuit.

A **product liability case** occurs after a consumer claims to be injured in some manner by a product. It is instructive to look at different types of torts which provide examples of potential liability claims. A tort, however, need not necessarily be covered by an insurance policy. Generally speaking, a **tort** is a civil wrong which unfairly causes loss or harm to another person. Tort claims take three forms: strict liability, intentional, or negligence. A strict liability claim arises when a company breaches its absolute obligation to make something safe. These claims typically involve medical malpractice or product liability. The plaintiff in a product liability claim, for example, need only prove that the event in question occurred and that the company's product or actions were responsible for the event. In contrast, intentional tort claims arise when the defending party actually intended to cause harm, or where it was reasonably foreseeable that harm would occur. Assault and invasion of privacy are examples of intentional torts. The most common type of tort claim is negligence, which is caused by a company breaching its duty to exercise a reasonable standard of care. Premise liability claims, for example, usually allege negligence on the part of the property owners and their agents. Negligence claims can also involve negligent hiring and retention, which occurs when an employer fails to conduct a proper background check on an employee, or fails to discipline an employee who later causes harm to someone else. From the standpoint of conducting an investigation into alleged negligence, a good starting point is first verifying that the event did, in fact, occur as alleged by the claimant. Then determine the extent of any willful intent or any breach of an established standard of care. Determining the prevalent standard of care related to a particular claim may require talking to others in the same industry, or hiring an expert to explain how others in the same industry would have acted under similar circumstances.

For example, since most private investigation companies perform background checks on their prospective employees as both a sound business practice and as the prevalent standard of care in the industry, if a company were to fail to perform a background check on an employee who had a prior assault conviction, and who subsequently assaults a customer, then the customer might file a tort claim against the company alleging negligent hiring. The insurance company holding the investigative company's insurance policy might conduct its own investigation to determine if the claim is consistent with the terms of the policy.

Many other types of insurance claims do not involve alleged negligence; they merely involve the unlucky events that often happen in life. These may include accidents, illnesses, and acts of nature, such as floods and tornados. These claims normally do not require any investigation, unless it is likely the damage or injuries were staged to avoid an exclusion not covered by the policy. For example, after Hurricane Katrina struck New Orleans in 2005, there were reports that homeowners who suffered property damage—but did not have flood or hurricane insurance—deliberately burned down their homes to make claims on existing fire insurance policies.[26] If true, this is an example of a claimant manipulating an insurance policy to be paid under an exclusion.

One case investigated by my firm involved a man, William, who was allegedly smoking a cigarette on an apartment balcony in Arlington, Virginia, when he leaned on the railing, somehow fell four stories, broke his leg, and sustained a concussion. William's injuries were not in question, as he had been transported to the emergency room after the fall and received immediate medical treatment, remaining in the hospital for two days. Because of the sustained injuries, William, who was attending school in England, had to prolong his visit to the United States by several weeks until he was well enough to travel. After returning to England, William filed a travel insurance claim with a British insurance company to be reimbursed for his medical and travel-related expenses incurred during the accident. His hotel bills and airfare alone—he stayed at a five star hotel while recovering in D.C.—cost over $10,000.

The insurance company was suspicious of the claim because they did not believe it likely that someone could fall from a fourth floor balcony and survive. They also did not understand, given that William claimed only to be leaning on the railing, how he fell from the balcony to begin with. The insurance company's investigators had already reviewed William's medical records related to the fall, and a notation describing him as "intoxicated" further perked their suspicions. Had William's fall actually been caused by his impairment due to alcohol or drugs, this would have constituted an exclusion, meaning the insurance company would not have been liable for paying the claim. The objective then involved determining exactly what happened when William fell from the balcony, so that the insurance company could resolve the claim consistent with the existing policy.

Unfortunately, aside from the cryptic notation on the medical records, no toxicology screen had been performed on William, so the real extent of his intoxication was unknown. Because nothing was structurally wrong with the balcony, and the height of the railing was in compliance with the building code, our investigation hinged on the circumstances surrounding the fall. Our hypothesis was that William's fall was caused by excessive alcohol consumption and possibly drug use. I began the investigation by canvassing the apartment complex for witnesses to the fall, intentionally avoiding Janet until near the end of the investigation. [The key to canvassing for witnesses is going to the scene around the same time of day, and preferably on the same day of the week, as when the event under investigation occurred. It is also important to canvass as soon as possible following an event, as witnesses' memories degrade quickly and they become less willing to cooperate as the novelty of the event wears off.] I ran database searches before beginning the canvass so that I knew the names of each home's occupants before leaving my office. For every resident who was not home at the time of my first canvass, I placed a note on the door with my business card, requesting that the resident call me to schedule an appointment. With patience and persistence, I was eventually able to speak with all the residents that had a reasonable chance of witnessing the fall.

While I was waiting for residents to call me back to schedule an appointment, I contacted the medical transport company that brought William to the hospital. I asked to speak with the two EMT employees who transported William. After I faxed William's signed medical release, authorizing us to investigate the claim on behalf of the insurance company, a manager from the medical transport company granted my interview request. I then went to their office in Fredericksburg, Virginia, and interviewed the two employees. Unfortunately, they did not remember William, even after I showed medical records that bore their signatures. Although it had been only a month since William's fall, given the fact that nearly one hundred ambulance runs were conducted in the interim, I found it plausible that the two employees simply did not remember this particular event. Finding them credible and without motive to lie, I continued to search for witnesses at the apartment complex.

Not surprisingly, given the time of day the event occurred, most of the residents I spoke to had not witnessed the fall. However, one woman, Julie, who responded to my note sounded very promising on the telephone, saying that she lived immediately downstairs from Janet and remembered the incident well. I scheduled an appointment to meet with Julie at her apartment the next evening. Because the layout of her living room was far from ideal for an investigative interview, I asked her if we could speak in her kitchen and she agreed. This allowed me to more accurately gauge her truthfulness as she relayed what she had witnessed. Regarding the event, Julie told me that she heard yelling outside and looked out her window to see a man's legs dangling from the balcony above her window. She said the man was singing in an English accent—and appeared to be under the influence of drugs or alcohol. I was careful to separate Julie's opinion about the degree to which the man was impaired from what she actually observed. For example, I elicited the tangible characteristics that supported her underlying belief—in this case, that William's speech was heavily slurred and that he was acting irrationally. She said that he appeared to be hanging onto the railing, before dropping down to the ground below. She said that she ran to her own railing and looked down, where she saw the man lying on the ground, two stories beneath her. She then heard a woman's voice above her, and looked up to see her neighbor, Janet, looking down at the man. According to Julie, Janet called to the man, "Stay there Bill! I'm calling an ambulance!" Julie said that she then continued making dinner. She said that a few days after the fall, she ran into Janet in the elevator and asked how the man was doing, to which Julie replied that he was okay but had just been "really drunk." The information supplied by Julie was helpful, not only because it supported the case's hypothesis, but also because it helped answer one of the mysteries that spurred the investigation in the first place: How did William survive a four-story fall with only a broken leg and a concussion? Because William was dangling from the balcony when he fell, according to Julie, the distance of the fall was decidedly less, closer to three stories.

With this information, I was finally ready to interview Janet. I called her to schedule an appointment at her apartment. When I arrived at Janet's apartment, she immediately seemed a little too phony and flirtatious. She complimented my suit and tie, asked if I worked out, and commented that being a private investigator must be a really great job. Given her behavior, and what Julie had told me, I suspected that Janet had something to hide. Regarding the incident, Janet told me that she had been taking a shower when her friend fell from the balcony. She said that he had two beers—but no more—and that he was acting normal. She said that when she got out of the shower she looked for William, but could not find him in her apartment. She then noticed the balcony door was open, which is when she went outside, looked down, and noticed William splayed out on the ground below. Asked if anyone else had witnessed the fall, Janet conspicuously failed to mention Julie—an example of withholding relevant information. Janet's responses were also tainted with unrealistic qualifiers, latent responses, significant postural shifts, and adaptive gestures. In other words, her story was behaviorally and factually problematic. I carefully got her to describe the beers William drank, what she was wearing when she went out on the balcony (a towel, she claimed), and other details of her story. I then had her sign a verbatim handwritten statement swearing under oath that these events were true, essentially locking her into her story.

After scheduling a follow-up interview with Julie, where I had her sign a typed declaration swearing to what she witnessed, I called Janet and asked her to come to my office to review and clarify her previous statement. Because of her flirtatious behavior at the apartment, I thought it wise to have a female investigator witness the interrogation. Janet insisted on bringing a male friend with her to the meeting, but I told her that her friend would have to wait in the lobby. Once in my office, Janet sat in a chair in front of my desk and I sat opposite her, such that we were four to six feet apart with no barriers between us. My female investigator, meanwhile, sat behind my desk, outside of Janet's field of vision. I was very careful to not sit between Janet and the exit to my office, in case she wanted to quit the interview for any reason.

I opened the interrogation by stating directly that my investigation had determined that she had not been truthful about the circumstances regarding William's fall. Such an accusation is the major element distinguishing an interview from an **interrogation**. Interrogations call for establishing a theme that leads to an alternative question posing two scenarios. Each scenario is an admission of guilt—in this case, an admission that she lied to me—but one response paints the subject in a somewhat more favorable light. Since I was ultimately trying to get Janet to admit knowledge of William's intoxication and possible drug use, I went with a knowledge-based theme, specifically attempting to minimize Janet's involvement as only having knowledge, versus being the primary culprit, in the insurance fraud.[27] In attempting to get her to confess this knowledge, I disclosed to her some of my evidence that was inconsistent with what she had told me in her earlier statement. Specifically, I told Janet that a neighbor had informed me that she was wearing a red sweater on the balcony, not a towel as she had claimed. After steadfastly discouraging her denials and persisting with the theme, I posed the alternative question to Janet, who finally admitted that she lied in her previous statement. She said that William had consumed approximately seven beers before he "fell" from the balcony. She maintained that she did not see him fall, however, saying that she only lied because she thought the fall was an accident and had nothing to do with the alcohol. But with Julie's declaration and Janet's inconsistent prior statement, I did not need Janet to admit this part.

I had Janet sign a typed declaration correcting her previous verbatim statement, making sure to include that she witnessed William drink seven beers within a three-hour period. In interpreting the data gleaned during the investigation, I determined that we had satisfactorily proved the hypothesis. This was the conclusion of the investigation.

Discussion: *Assume that William's fall had not been a simple medical insurance claim, but rather a negligence tort filed against the building owners. In what ways would the investigation have been different? When interviewing the EMT workers, what is an example of a hypothetical question that might have locked them into an account consistent with the hypothesis? What are some alternative questions that might have resulted in Janet admitting her knowledge that William drank more than two beers on the night of the incident?*

15

Domestic Investigations

Domestic investigations involve interfamily matters, such as issues relevant to divorce, custody disputes, and probate cases. Investigations into probate matters involve attempting to prove or disprove the intentions of a deceased person on behalf of an heir, and sometimes even involves locating heirs of an estate. I recall one case where we tracked down all the employees of a bank where a will's signature had been notarized nearly a decade earlier. The bank had changed owners three times within that timeframe and had eventually closed. Our client, the would-be heir to a sizable inheritance, wanted to discover if any of the bank's ex-employees had known the deceased and could testify about her state of mind when she signed the will.

Domestic cases involving locating a missing heir are typically paid with funds drawn from the estate, and usually involve conducting simple database searches to locate relatives who may not have had contact with the deceased for quite some time. One case that we worked involved locating the son, and sole heir, of a family estate. The son had killed his mother in the United States and had been declared legally insane, and therefore not culpable for the crime. He was extradited to France, and, when his father died nearly twenty years later without leaving a will, he was entitled to the entire, very substantial estate. An investigator at our firm located the son in a Paris slum, but the man, still psychotic, was convinced that the investigator had come to arrest him. He therefore refused to cooperate. The man's paranoia ended up costing him a lofty inheritance.

Most domestic investigations involve divorce and custody disputes. Cases intended to prove infidelity are especially common in the private investigative industry. It is generally considered unethical to conduct infidelity investigations for parties who are not married. In other words, private investigators should not accept cases on behalf of boyfriends or girlfriends who just "want to know" if their lover is cheating on them, as this is tantamount to stalking. In many states, including Virginia, infidelity is one legal basis of an at-fault divorce, which can afford the other party a greater share of the marital equity or attorney's fees, or more money in spousal support. Divorce is the only legitimate reason to conduct an infidelity investigation. To become divorced in Virginia, the husband and wife must live separated for six months or twelve months, depending on whether either party has children. Infidelity is only relevant as a factor for the court's consideration, however, if it occurred prior to the date of separation.

Most infidelity investigations involve conducting surveillance on the subject and trying to catch him on video in the act of being unfaithful. This is generally not as easy or sexy as it sounds. Surveillance is very time intensive and requires either a substantial budget or "getting lucky" by being at the right place at the right time. Information obtained from the subject's emails, mobile phone records, and social media data provided by the client can be very helpful in determining the most likely place to catch infidelity in the act. However, an investigator must never suggest that a client access the spouse's personal records unless those records are held in joint accounts with the client.

Viewing a subject in the company of someone of the opposite sex is not sufficient to prove unfaithfulness, and cheaters who are married are rarely careless enough to engage in public displays of affection. Luckily, establishing infidelity only requires reaching the threshold of a preponderance of the evidence. Usually these cases are made by anecdotal evidence, such as video footage showing a female subject entering a man's home and not leaving for several hours. This can be accomplished by documenting the time that the woman arrived, observing the exits of the home, and then documenting the time that she left. [Investigators sometimes place a small wedge of paper between the door and door jamb, or a penny on top of a car tire to verify that the subject did not leave when direct observation is not possible.] A woman who, for example, spends the night at a male acquaintance's home, or who is observed going into a motel room with him, can generally be found to have been unfaithful by a preponderance of the evidence (generally described as a fifty-one percent certainty). Other evidence that may be sufficient to prove infidelity includes video evidence of kissing, hand holding, and other behavior that is indicative of an intimate relationship.

Custody cases are generally more diverse and complicated than those involving infidelity. The issues under investigation can vary from alleged abuse and neglect, to the violation of various court orders and agreements. Parties in divorce cases sometimes hire private investigators to obtain evidence of unsuitability to have custody of children. Such evidence might include illegal behavior, heavy drinking or drug use, or contact with unsavory individuals who might put the children at risk. The most important factors in determining custody are the safety and wellbeing of the children. In cases where a child may have been abused or neglected, the court will intervene and assign a **guardian ad litem**, usually a private attorney, who is tasked with representing the best interests of the child.

Our firm was once hired by the Washington, D.C. office of a national law firm that was representing a young child, age five, who was living with her maternal grandmother in southeast quadrant of the city. The child's mother was arrested for child abuse, and the court ordered her to stay away from the child post-incarceration.[28] After a person identified as a "neighbor" made an anonymous complaint to the D.C. Child and Family Service Agency (CFSA) that the grandmother, Jill, was using and selling drugs from the apartment where the child was staying—and that her son, Robert, the child's uncle and a convicted murderer, was also staying at the home—the appointed guardian ad litem, an attorney at the law firm, retained us to investigate the allegations. The stated problem of the case was the need to gather evidence that could be used in a family court proceeding to either substantiate or refute the anonymous complaint.

Because of the danger possibly posed to the child in this case, and because the law firm was working on the case pro bono, I decided that it was appropriate for our firm to significantly discount our fee. After having the law firm sign a contract, I assigned the preliminary investigation to our associate investigator, Steve, who conducted database inquiries on all the occupants in the building, which consisted of two apartments. Once he had the names of everyone associated with the building, he then used the same database to run address histories for each individual. Once Steve had the address histories, he then searched for their criminal records within the respective jurisdictions. Conducting criminal records searches in Washington, D.C. at that time required Steve to physically go to the criminal clerk's office on the fourth floor of D.C. Superior Court. Steve's report provided the name and contact information of the building's landlord, the names and criminal histories of four people associated with the apartment, and the name of the neighbor in the second apartment, who may have been responsible for making the anonymous compliant. It also confirmed that Robert had recently been paroled and appeared to be living in the apartment.

We decided that testing the hypothesis in this case—substantiating the anonymous complaint—required a two-pronged approach: conducting fixed surveillance on the residence for signs of possible drug activity, and interviewing the landlord and neighbors who may have made the complaint. Since conducting interviews might have tipped off Jill that she was under investigation, we decided to first conduct two weeks of surveillance before making contact with witnesses. Neighborhood surveillance was difficult because it was a high-drug area and ethnically homogeneous; a place where a white male sitting alone in a vehicle was likely to draw attention. Because of the potential safety issues, I decided to conduct the surveillance personally; I did not want to put an employee at risk when I was available to conduct the surveillance myself. My vehicle was a Nisan Altima with tinted windows, not a car likely to arouse suspicion. With a state-of-the-art digital video camera allowing me to observe the building from approximately seventy-five yards away, it was unlikely that I would get burned.

Surveying the neighborhood, I determined there were two ideal vantage points; one was located about seventy-five yards away from the building up on a hill, and the other was located about thirty yards from the building on the opposite side. The first location was preferable during the daytime because it afforded an optimum view of the front of the building with little risk of being seen by Jill or anyone who would inform her of my presence. The location was problematic in the evening, however, because it was difficult to see the subjects' faces using night vision at a distance of seventy-five yards. The second location was on the same side of the street as Jill's building and across a major intersection, far too close for daytime surveillance but ideal for nighttime surveillance when my vehicle would be partially masked by traffic. From the second vantage point I could clearly see the subjects entering and exiting the apartment.

I took these two positions in four-hour increments periodically over the following two weeks, alternating between daytime and nighttime surveillance, and videotaping all the activity near the apartment. I also followed Jill and the child as they walked to the child's nearby kindergarten, in order to make sure she was being treated properly. Altogether, there was some suspicious activity, such as cars that stopped in front of the building and groups of people that walked into the alley behind the building for periods of time. One night, the police stopped a group of young people standing in front of the building and I observed them using flashlights to search the front yard. They were looking for bags of drugs that may have been jettisoned as the police approached. The police never made an arrest. Throughout the surveillance, I carefully zoomed in on the face of each subject who entered and exited the apartment, the police officers who conducted the stop, and the tags of all relevant vehicles. Ultimately, however, the two weeks of surveillance did not uncover any definitive proof of drug activity. I printed still photographs of the people I observed, including Robert, who was definitely living at the home. Then we moved to the next step in the observation and experimentation phase of the investigation; the interviews.

I assigned Steve to interview the landlord, who lived in Maryland, and I interviewed the neighbors and police officers who conducted the stop during my surveillance. The landlord described Jill as a model tenant. He said that he had received no complaints about drug activity in his building, and he disavowed knowledge of anyone else living in the apartment. The interview was still helpful, however, because the landlord informed Steve that the occupants of the two apartments did not get along and had frequent disagreements about the noise level. In fact, he was in the process of evicting the neighbor, in part because of complaints made to him by Jill. This provided a possible motive for the neighbor to have complained to CFSA on behalf of the child.

When I approached the neighbor, Wanda, she refused steadfastly to cooperate or to acknowledge that it was she who made the complaint. My sense was that Wanda feared retaliation from Robert. I then went to the police department and requested to speak to the officer who had participated in the stop I observed. The degree that police officers will cooperate with a private investigation depends on the purpose of the investigation. Those working for criminal defendants will often find police officers uncooperative and sometimes outright hostile. Since this was an investigation intended to get a young child out of a potentially dangerous environment, Officer John ultimately agreed to speak with me. Officer John identified Robert from the still photographs obtained from my surveillance and confirmed that police suspected, but could not confirm, that Jill and Robert were selling drugs from the apartment.

After interpreting the data—the information provided by Officer John, coupled with my surveillance video showing suspicious activity outside the apartment—the judge swiftly removed the child from the grandmother's home on the advice of the guardian ad litem and placed her with a foster family pending a thorough investigation by CFSA. Interestingly, Jill did not fight the judge's decision and therefore waived custody, possibly because she realized the added scrutiny would cut off her only other source of income.

Discussion: What are some ways that an investigator could establish that infidelity occurred prior to a marital separation? The above custody investigation primarily employed research, covert surveillance, and interviews to test the hypothesis. What other methods might have been used to test the hypothesis?

16

Accident Investigations

Private investigators are often tasked with investigating accidents, which can involve cars, boats, bicycles, motorcycles, and even pedestrians. These cases are typically initiated by insurance companies, although investigators sometimes work for plaintiffs in helping to prosecute negligence or strict liability tort claims.[29] As with all investigations, interviewing the client, whether he is the plaintiff or the defendant, is essential to a full understanding of what happened from his perspective. Following the client interview, the investigator next obtains and reviews the police accident report (if the accident was reported to the police), and the medical records of any injured parties. Accident reports are generally public information, obtainable by contacting the applicable police department and requesting a copy of the report. These reports often list the names and addresses of the parties to the accident, as well as all witnesses. Medical reports are obtained by release in the case of insurance investigations, and through discovery during cases involving litigation.

The investigator will then photograph and diagram the area of the alleged accident and attempt to interview witnesses to the event. In visiting the scene of an accident, the investigator will attempt to determine the consistency of the scene's layout with the parties' accounts of what occurred. Although it takes an expert in accident reconstruction to conduct a full analysis and to testify as an expert witness, an investigator can often identify inconsistencies by examining the scene and any vehicles involved. The key to accident cases involving vehicles is the issue of right-of-way, because this will determine who acted with negligence by violating the prevailing rules of road (or maritime rules, etc.). These rules vary depending on who had the red, yellow, or green light, and sometimes depend on the relative position of the involved vehicles.

Aside from the witnesses listed on the accident report, the investigator may locate additional witnesses by canvassing businesses and homes near the scene. Canvassing must be done soon after the accident occurred, because witnesses' memories deteriorate quickly.

Another element of investigating accidents is an investigation of the opposing party's alleged injuries. This is typically accomplished through covert surveillance of the subject to ascertain whether he is violating disclosed medical restrictions. Video that shows a subject engaged in activities that should be precluded by the nature of his alleged injuries is a powerful piece of evidence that may be used to impeach the witness's credibility.

One investigation conducted by our firm involved a lawsuit against a vehicle manufacturer. In this case, four teenagers, between ages 17 and 19, were driving in a brand new car on a rainy day when they veered off the road and smashed head-on into a streetlamp pole. The car had been a high school graduation present for the driver. All the young men were wearing seatbelts, and no alcohol or other vehicles were involved in the accident. According to the police report, the car was traveling no more than thirty miles per hour at the time it hit the pole. This appeared to be a case of a relatively inexperienced driver losing traction on the slick road, skidding sideways, and then overcompensating by turning the steering wheel too hard in the opposite direction, thereby losing control and driving into the pole. Despite the relatively slow speed of the crash, the car was deemed a total loss by the driver's insurance company and was forfeited in return for the insurance payment, minus the deductible.

Although three of the young men did not suffer major injuries, one backseat passenger, Justin, sustained a major back injury that required extensive surgery. The doctors opined that Justin would only be able to walk again after a year of physical therapy. Prior to the accident, the injured young man had received a full scholarship to a top university as a figure skater, and he was a serious candidate for the U.S. Olympic figure skating team. Because Justin was wearing his seatbelt during the accident and was in excellent physical condition, his parents could not understand how his injuries had been so extensive. Suspecting that Justin's seatbelt did not function properly, they decided to hire an experienced lawyer to investigate any defects. The lawyer retained our firm, along with an expert, John, who had twenty years' experience reconstructing accidents, to examine the vehicle. The stated problem of the case was to determine if Justin's injuries were caused by a material defect in the vehicle. The hypothesis was that a defect existed in the car's seatbelt.

By the time Justin's family hired the lawyer, nearly four months had passed since the accident. After thoroughly interviewing Justin, our assigned investigator, Sheila, immediately obtained the accident report from the police department and traveled to the scene of the accident to photograph and diagram the scene with John. Sheila took hundreds of photographs in a coordinated series from the general to the specific, starting far from the streetlamp pole, which had been repaired since the accident, and working her way up to the area around the pole, looking for any real evidence left behind as she went. Together with John, Sheila measured all the relevant distances, using triangulation to measure freestanding objects such as the streetlamp pole in relation to other objects. Skid marks were still visible where the vehicle entered the median where the streetlamp pole was located. This evidence provided important clues regarding how the vehicle must have struck the pole. To later prove that the skid marks were actually caused by the vehicle in this crash, Sheila used a pocket knife to scrape some of the rubber and cement into a plastic bag, making sure to carefully document when and where the evidence was collected. Once the flakes of rubber and debris were inside the bag, she taped the bag shut and signed her full name over the tape to establish the beginning of the chain of custody. This evidence could later be tested to match the tires on the vehicle in the crash. The exact location of the skid marks and their particular characteristics could be used by John to establish the estimated speed and trajectory of the vehicle prior to impact. When Sheila returned to our office, she created a formal sketch of the entire scene for later use as a demonstrative exhibit during trial.

Sheila next interviewed the three young men who had also been in the vehicle. Two of the interviews were conducted at the witnesses' respective homes, but she had to do the third interview over the telephone, since this witness, the driver, was away at college. For each interview, Sheila took copious notes and prepared formal reports documenting their accounts, which were credible and wholly consistent. After providing each report to our client, she again contacted each witness and had him sign a declaration. For the driver, who was away at college, Sheila reviewed the declaration via telephone and then hired a local investigator to bring the declaration to his dorm for signature. The reason Sheila did not email the declaration to the driver was because the declaration was so vital to the case that she did not want to jeopardize the driver signing the document.

Sheila then attempted to find the car, which the insurance company had previously sold at auction. She determined the car was at a scrap yard in Baltimore, and she called the scrap company to make arrangements to view the car with John. At the scrap yard, Sheila took hundreds of photographs of the car, inside and out, while John examined the seat belt. Suspecting a defect in the centrifugal clutch, but being unable to sufficiently examine the mechanism at the scrap yard, John requested that they purchase the vehicle and have it towed back to his garage for careful disassembly and examination. However, Sheila was told by the scrap company that most of the still operable parts were pledged to another buyer. Therefore, the scrap company could not sell the vehicle to Sheila and John. Since the competence of John's potential testimony about the seatbelt might be called into question, Sheila offered to have John remove the mechanism at the scrap yard himself. But the scrap company refused to allow John to take apart the seat belt mechanism, citing concerns about liability, should John get hurt on their property.

Sheila bargained persistently with the owner of the scrap yard and finally got him to agree to a solution: for $500 the scrap yard would cut the vehicle in half and allow Sheila to take the half that she needed. By hiring a tow truck company to retrieve the rear half of the vehicle, this solution would preserve the evidence, which could then be delivered to John's garage for closer examination. Sheila continually snapped photographs while a worker sawed the car in half using the diamond-tipped blade of a Stihl saw. She then followed the tow truck to John's garage, where she had John sign a chain of custody form. She was sure to record the full names of both the worker who sawed the car in half and the tow truck driver, and she carefully documented each stage of the operation in case the defense alleged that any defect in the seat belt was caused by the saw, the transport of the vehicle, or another factor unrelated to the accident. By remaining with the vehicle until it was securely in John's custody, Sheila could confidently testify that nothing unusual happened to the car that would have affected the seat belt mechanism.

After interpreting the data documented by Sheila and John, it was concluded that Justin's injuries were, in fact, likely the result of a faulty centrifugal clutch. The automobile company offered a substantial settlement, which Justin and his family accepted. Although he would never be an Olympian, Justin would be able to go to college for free and live a relatively normal life after his recovery period.

Discussion: What methods did Sheila use during the observation and experimentation phase of the investigation? Had the investigative firm been hired by the insurance company or the automobile company, how might Sheila's methods have been different? Why was it important for Sheila to obtain the names of the workers involved with cutting and transporting the vehicle?

Notes

1. Due diligence, in a similar but distinct context, also refers to verifying the assets and liabilities of a business entity. This commonly occurs prior to a merger or acquisition.

2. The first step of the scientific method is to state the problem, which is discussed in Chapter 3. The subsequent steps of the scientific method are to form the hypothesis, observe and experiment, interpret the data, and draw conclusions.

3. The names of our employees and all other parties have been changed in the case examples provided.

4. Many federal laws, such as the Age Discrimination in Employment Act, the Family Medical Leave Act, and Title VII of the Civil Rights Act of 1964, require employers to keep records related to hiring decisions for certain periods of time, usually two or three years. The length of time that a particular employer must maintain records depends on the size of the organization.

5. Fair Credit Reporting Act 15 U.S.C. § 1681 et seq.

6. There is more detail about the use of investigative databases in Chapter 4.

7. Fair Credit Reporting Act 15 U.S.C. § 1681 et seq.

8. Horwitz, Sari; Higham, Scott; and Moreno, Sylvia (07/24/08). "Who Killed Chandra Levy?" *The Washington Post*.

9. U.S.C. Title 18, Part II, Chapter 201 § 3006 A

10. For information on how to become a certified CJA investigator in Washington, D.C., visit www.dcpds.org. My business partner, Brendan Wells, created and operates the training program, and I have been a guest speaker on several occasions. The twenty-hour class is highly informative for those interested in conducting criminal defense investigations—and it is free!

11. Evidence will be discussed in Part V (The Law of Investigations).

12. Wells, Gary L. & Olson, Elizabeth A. "Eyewitness Testimony." *Annual Review of Psychology*: 01/01/03.

13. Nakashima, Ellen & Noguchi, Yuki (10/5/06). "Dunn, Four Others Charges in Hewlett Surveillance Case." *The Washington Post*: A01.

14. Telephone Records and Privacy Protection Act of 2006, Public Law 109–476

15. Virginia Code § 18.2-186.3

16. The Federal Identity Theft Assumption and Deterrence Act of 1974, 18 U.S. Code 47 § 1028, for example, prohibits producing or displaying false national, foreign government, or quasi-governmental identification documents.

17. There is some debate in the investigative industry about the scope of the term "confidential telephone information" and whether it covers only call detail records, which have a high expectation of privacy, or whether it also includes telephone subscriber information, where the expectation of privacy is less.

18. Gramm-Leach-Bliley Act (1999), 15 U.S.C. § 6821

19. Aryanpur, Arianne (4/30/06). "Human Trafficking Hits Home; Activists Say Crime Isn't Just a Foreign Problem, Urge Action," *The Washington Post*: C-12.

20. Sarbanes-Oxley Act of 2002, Public Law 107-204, 106 Stat. 745

21. False Claims Act (1863), 31 U.S.C 3729-3733

22. Code of Virginia, 18.2 § 460

23. McCool, Grant and Graybow, Martha (03/13/09). "Madoff Pleads Guilty, Is Jailed for $65 Billion Fraud." *The Washington Post*: A-01.

24. Telephone Records and Privacy Protection Act of 2006, Public Law 109-476

25. DeStafano, Todd (2002). "Insurance Fraud and the Defense Attorney." In *Corporate Investigations* (Montgomery, Reginald and Majeski, William, editors). Lawyers and Judges Publishing: Tucson, AZ, pp. 569-590.

26. Media release from the Insurance Information Institute (04/09). Retrieved from www.iii.org/media/hottopics/insurance/fraud/ on 04/04/09.

27. For an excellent treatise on interrogation themes, see Senese, Louis (2005). *Anatomy of Interrogation Themes: The Reid Technique of Interviewing and Interrogation*. John E. Reid & Associates: Chicago, IL.

28. The applicable law that prevents the disclosure of facts pertaining to this case is DC Code § 4.1303.06. The facts herein have been highly fictionalized to protect confidentiality.

29. Ritter, Frank (2006). *Successful Personal Injury Investigations: Master the Techniques of Finding the Facts that Win Cases*. Diverse Publications; Oceanside, California.

Part V

The Law of Investigations

17

The Law of Private Investigations

Privacy and Employment Law

There are many specific laws that relate directly or indirectly to the work of private investigators, including state and federal privacy regulations and laws protecting employees whom investigators may encounter during their investigations. Relevant federal privacy legislation includes the Electronic Communications Privacy Act, the Privacy Act of 1974, the Telephone Records and Privacy Protection Act of 2006, the Gramm-Leach-Blily Act, the Fair Credit Reporting Act, the Fair Debt Collection Practices Act, the Freedom of Information Act, and the Computer Fraud and Abuse Act. Pertinent employment laws include the rules for *ex parte* contact of witnesses; the decision in *National Labor Relations Board v. Weingarten*; the Civil Rights Acts of 1866, 1964, and 1991; the Rehabilitation Act of 1973; the Americans with Disabilities Act of 1990; the Family and Medical Leave Act; and laws protecting whistleblowers, such as the Sarbanes-Oxley Act.

One critical area of privacy is in the conduction of audio recording and wiretapping. In this area, Title III of the Omnibus Crime Control and Safe Streets Act of 1968[1] dealt with many issues relevant to criminal justice and law enforcement, one of which was the codification of federal wiretap laws after the *Katz* case, which conceptualized privacy rights that do not apply specifically to property. The applicable section of the law that addressed this issue was the **Electronic Communications Privacy Act (ECPA)**,[2] which was passed as an amendment to Title III in 1986. The ECPA protects all wire, oral, and electronic communications within the United States from government intrusion. The ECPA was modified to some extent by the USA Patriot Act,[3] passed in late 2001 following the 9/11 terrorist attacks. The USA Patriot Act allows federal agents to issue so-called "national security letters" to retrieve certain communications, instead of requiring a court order. Still, the ECPA remains the law that dictates how all phone and Internet communications must be obtained by investigators in terms of the duration and scope of the recordings. The law does not prohibit the intrusion into areas where there is a decidedly lesser degree of privacy, such as with telephone metadata that does not include the actual *content* of the calls or emails. Telephone metadata is analogous to the caller identification feature available for most telephone subscribers in the United States; it includes the names of parties to incoming and outgoing communications to a particular telephone or Internet account, as well as when, and sometimes where, the parties were at the time of the message. It does not include the actual content of the communications.

In the private sector, intercepting private communications must only be done with the consent of one party to the communication, and in some states (e.g., Maryland) *all* parties must consent to the interception. Wiretapping or hacking into email accounts is therefore strictly prohibited. In the past, many private investigators obtained telephone call records analogous to telephone metadata by pretexting telephone service providers. Essentially, they would contact the telephone company and pretend to be the subscriber to the phone number under investigation and, by claiming to have questions about the bill, would obtain the call detail records for the account. This practice was banned with the passing of the **Telephone Records and Privacy Protection Act of 2006 (Telephone Privacy Act)**.[4] Specifically, the Telephone Privacy Act bans telephone and Internet pretexting, as well as the receipt and transfer of the associated information. The act defines covered confidential telephone information as that which:

- Relates to the quantity, technical configuration, type, destination, location, or amount of use of a service offered by a covered entity, subscribed to by any customer of that covered entity, and kept by or on behalf of that covered entity solely by virtue of the relationship between that covered entity and the customer;
- Is made available to a covered entity by a customer solely by virtue of the relationship between that covered entity and the customer; or

- Is contained in any bill, itemization, or account statement provided to a customer by or on behalf of a covered entity solely by virtue of the relationship between that covered entity and the customer.[5]

Some private investigators maintain that confidential telephone information does not include subscriber information, such as a customer's name and address. Under this interpretation, investigators could still pretext telephone numbers to learn the identity of a subscriber or to learn the telephone number or address of a subject. This interpretation has not yet been tested in court. Since the Telephone Privacy Act carries a maximum penalty of ten years in prison, it is unlikely that private investigators will exercise this interpretation. Furthermore, it should be noted that the Federal Trade Commission (FTC) holds that the sale of *any* confidential information obtained via pretext violates the Federal Trade Commission Act, which bans unfair or deceptive trade practices.[6] Therefore, investigators should only pretext subscriber information at their own peril. What is clear, however, is that obtaining telephone call and email records always requires a subpoena in the private sector.

Prior to the Telephone Privacy Act, the only explicit federal statutory ban on pretexting was the **Gramm-Leach-Bliley Act (GLBA)**, which bans the use of misrepresentation while gathering confidential information from financial institutions,[7] including insurance companies, credit card issuers, and consumer reporting agencies (e.g., the credit bureaus). The prohibitions of the law do not apply to fraud investigations conducted by insurance institutions and their agents, or to child support investigations conducted by licensed private investigators—provided that a court has adjudged the subject to be in arrears on his child support obligations, and the efforts of the investigator are "reasonably necessary" to effect collection.[8] The GLBA also regulates the use of financial information obtained legitimately from financial institutions, setting forth several permissible purposes for access to this information. Whenever a private investigator accesses a consumer investigative report, often referred to as conducting a database search, she is expressly attesting that her reason for accessing this information conforms to these GLBA permissible purposes, which include investigating or preventing fraud, and investigations related to civil and criminal litigation. Sometimes database companies have the investigative business sign disclosures up front, acknowledging that they will only access information in compliance with GLBA; other times the database companies require an acknowledgment of compliance at each log-in into the website in order to access the search engine.

Another law that carefully regulates the use of consumer information, including financial and credit information, is the **Fair Credit Reporting Act (FCRA)**.[9] The section of that FCRA most relevant to investigators is that which governs the use of so-called consumer reports, which the law defines as any report pertaining to a subject's character and general reputation. Under this nebulous definition, many reports prepared by private investigators, especially those prepared regarding internal investigations conducted on behalf of companies and concerning the company's employees, would likely be consumer reports covered by the FCRA. The law does not generally pertain to private investigations related to the public or to investigations related to litigation. Under the FCRA, when a company hires an outside investigator to investigate an employee, they must first obtain the consent of the employee under investigation, and afterward provide that employee with a copy of the investigative report, provided the company intends to take any action based upon the information contained in the report. The requirement to notify employees of an impending investigation does not apply to investigations concerning alleged employee misconduct, violations of the law, or violations of any pre-existing employment policies. However, the notification requirement does apply during pre-employment background investigations, and, in any event where adverse action is taken against an employee related to *any* consumer report, the employer must provide a summary of the investigation to the employee and allow him the opportunity to contest the findings therein.

While the FCRA specifically regulates internal investigations in a workplace setting, other laws address how investigators must treat the public during other types of investigations. The **Fair Debt Collection Practices Act (FDCPA)**, for example, establishes many limitations for private investigators and other third parties involved in the collection of debt from consumers.[10] Pursuant to the FDCPA, private investigators must not:

- Attempt to contact a consumer after being notified in writing to stop;
- Contact a consumer at his place of employment after having been told not to do so, either verbally or in writing;
- Misrepresent facts or falsely threaten legal action against a consumer without the intent to do so;
- Contact a consumer known to be represented by counsel;

- Contact a consumer via telephone outside the hours of 8 a.m. and 9 p.m.

Federal law also regulates the information that may be maintained on private citizens and whom may access this information. The **Privacy Act of 1974** prohibits federal agencies from gathering certain information about citizens, including government employees and contractors, not necessary or relevant to the government agency's mission.[11] There are some exceptions, such as records maintained by the U.S. Census Bureau. The law allows citizens to review information collected about them, expounding upon the provisions of the **Freedom of Information Act (FOIA)**.[12] Public records laws also exist in most states, like the Virginia Freedom of Information Act that was modeled after the federal law.[13] FOIA and the similar state laws establish what information maintained by the government is available to the public. By submitting a formal letter of request to the applicable federal or state government agency, investigators may obtain copies of most government records, provided their release would not compromise national security or any active law enforcement investigation. Any information that is specific to an individual citizen, however, may only be obtained by an investigator with a subpoena, or with a release of information signed by the citizen who is the subject of the information.

There are also state and federal laws that protect the privacy and security of computer users. For example, the **Computer Fraud and Abuse Act** prohibits "exceeding authorized access" of someone's computer to obtain financial data, government records, or passwords.[14] Similarly, in Virginia it is illegal to examine, make unauthorized copies, alter, or destroy any computer data without the permission of the computer's owner. Virginia law also specifically bars the use of key-loggers intended to record the key strokes of computer users without the owner's permission.[15] Similar laws exist in most states.

In addition to these federal and state privacy laws, there are many rules that define the rights of employees who may be witnesses in employment investigations. When conducting internal investigations for employers, the subjects of the investigation (i.e., the employees) are generally compelled to cooperate with the investigation or face possible disciplinary actions by the employer, including termination. They have no right to have an attorney or witness present while being interviewed, save for union members who are only entitled to have a union representative present.[16] Even for union employees, however, the representative is not permitted to interfere with the questioning. Because of this formidable power that employers—and, by extension, their investigators—have over employees, there are many laws protecting employees from becoming the subjects of discrimination or retaliation during investigations. Ergo, from the standpoint of an investigator, internal investigations are potentially fraught with litigious pitfalls from these numerous employment laws protecting particular classes of employees. It is important to note that the rules discussed below are not inclusive of all relevant laws protecting employees during an investigation, and that protection often extends to employees who are mere witnesses to complaints made by their co-workers.

The most general and all-encompassing employment laws include the various Civil Rights Acts, particularly the Civil Rights Acts of 1866, 1964, and 1991, which collectively prevent discrimination in the workplace. Since an unreasonable investigation of an employee by a private investigator could be construed as a punitive measure intended to single out a subject in an unfair or disparate manner, investigators must be ever-conscious that their actions do not constitute illegal discrimination. The **Civil Rights Act of 1866** prohibits *intentional* discrimination based upon race or national origin, meaning that, for the investigator to run afoul of this law, she would have to intentionally single out employees based upon their protected status.[17] All companies and contractors in the United States are covered by this law, making it universally illegal to overtly discriminate on the basis of race or national origin. However, the **Civil Rights Act of 1964** expanded these protections to include color, religion, and sex, and it extended the definition of discrimination to include discriminatory practices that do not necessarily have a discriminatory intent.[18] Although the Civil Rights Act of 1964 only applies to companies with fifteen or more employees, those tasked with conducting investigations within these companies must take proactive measures to ensure the results of their investigations have no discriminatory *effect*, irrespective of what they actually intended. Furthermore, with the **Civil Rights Act of 1991**, the burden of proof for showing that investigative actions created a discriminatory environment shifted from the employee to the employer.[19] In other words, investigators working for companies with fifteen or more employees must go the extra mile to ensure their investigations are wholly unbiased and have no discriminatory effect.

Other classes of individuals are also protected from discrimination during workplace investigations. For example, the **Americans with Dis-**

abilities Act of 1990 (ADA)[20] and the **Rehabilitation Act of 1973**[21] prohibit discrimination against persons with disabilities, and the **Family and Medical Leave Act of 1993** protects employees who have exercised medical leave. The ADA, which only applies to companies with fifteen or more employees, requires those companies to make reasonable accommodations to compensate for an employee's disability. Investigators interviewing, or otherwise investigating disabled workers on behalf of their employers must similarly ensure that adequate accommodations are offered to these employees to prevent any undue hardships. The Rehabilitation Act, which only applies to companies that receive federal financial assistance, or who have federal contracts in excess of $2,500, defines covered disabilities to include individuals with drug and alcohol addiction. In other words, investigations involving illicit drugs or alcohol impairment at federal contractor sites may spur claims of discrimination against "handicapped [sic]" addicts.[22] The ADA, however, does not currently protect these individuals.

Lastly, the **Family and Medical Leave Act of 1993 (FMLA)**,[23] which only applies to companies with fifty or more employees, and only to employees who have worked at the company for one year, prohibits retaliation against employees for exercising medical leave. It is significant to note that many cases of fraud are discovered when a culprit has gone on medical leave, because it is only then that he can no longer control access to the instruments and methods of his fraud. Investigators conducting an investigation of an employee on FMLA leave, therefore, must be very careful not to consider the employee's absence or his underlying medical condition in the findings of the investigation.

It is important to note that the liability inherent in these and other laws protecting employees are only relevant to investigators working on behalf of employers. For investigators who are investigating companies and employees from the outside, or on behalf of some other interest (e.g., a plaintiff), the concerns are decidedly different. For example, when conducting an investigation regarding a company who is a party to litigation, there are rules that dictate the extent to which an investigator may contact certain current and former employees of that company. In Virginia, for example, an investigator is permitted to contact former employees of a company, provided the subject of the interview does not include privileged information. An investigator may contact current employees of an organization unless those employees have the authority to bind the company in the litigation. These employees, sometimes referred to as the control group or the alter egos of the company, include officers and other key employees of the organization. When working on behalf of an attorney, it is never permissible to contact an individual represented by counsel, unless the scope of the questioning is limited to public information.[24] This rule applies to all investigations.

> **Discussion:** *The FCRA requires employers to notify employees of the initiation of many types of investigations, with broad exceptions. What are some examples of cases that would require notification under the FCRA? What are some imperative principles and sound business practices that might help prevent an investigation from having a discriminating effect? For example, consider a theft investigation that involves an employee out on FMLA leave. How could an investigator ensure that the employee's medical condition, or the fact that he was absent, did not influence the outcome of the investigation?*

18

The Law of Public Investigations

State Action

This chapter discusses a number of constitutional restrictions placed on investigators. It is important to note that many aspects of the Constitution apply only to agents of the government, not to private individuals—including private investigators. This means that, essentially, a private investigator is not required to read subjects Miranda warnings, and evidence that she collects will typically not be excluded from trial on any constitutional ground, unless she can be deemed what is called a *state actor*, as the particular circumstances warrant. This is sometimes referred to as the *doctrine of state action*. Although this is not a well-litigated area (perhaps fortuitously), factors that can make a private investigator more likely to be considered a state actor include working at the explicit direction of the government, being given arrest authority afforded by the state, or functioning under government licensing and regulation. The use of badges, uniforms, guns, and other hallmarks of law enforcement are also common elements that can bestow the status of a state actor upon a private citizen. However, the courts have generally found that state action requires that the entity or individual in question be performing duties that have traditionally been reserved for law enforcement. The issue of state action is most likely to occur when a private investigator discovers evidence proffered by the government in a subsequent trial, which a criminal defendant in a criminal trial (or the party adverse to the government in civil litigation) wants to have excluded.

The Constitution and the Rule of Law

The *rule of law* is the concept in American society that the law reigns supreme over any person or group of people, from individuals, to corporations, to the President of the United States. Abiding by the rule of law is of integral importance for investigators in order to avoid falling into the trap of viewing the legal system as a purely adversarial process, or believing that the end can justify any means. On a philosophical level, the rule of law was initially conceived in the United States as the balancing system between the opposing forces of totalitarianism and anarchy. Think about the two as a scale along a continuum, with totalitarianism on one side and anarchy on another. On the one side, civilized societies require some mechanism with which to implement order, such as the authorization given to police to enforce criminal law, without which they fall further down the scale toward disorder, crime, and anarchy. On the other extreme, given unbridled power (e.g., the ability to conduct searches of all persons and property without limitation), the forces of order will impose totalitarianism, where individual freedom is grossly curtailed. The rule of law balances these opposing forces by setting forth the limitation of the power of law. As agents of the law in one form or another, it is important for investigators to have an appreciation for the limits and powers set forth under this doctrine in the United States.

The bedrock of the rule of law concept in the United States is the Constitution, drafted in 1787, and the accompanying Bill of Rights, which are the first ten amendments to the Constitution, ratified in 1791. Judicial decisions made by the Supreme Court in regards to constitutional questions are also an essential part of the canon of constitutional law. While the original draft of the U.S. Constitution is only approximately four pages long, the body of law that relates directly to the Constitution—and is therefore *an essential part* of the Constitution—could fill a legal library. The original articles and amendments of the Constitution cannot be modified, overruled, or abridged by any law, court action, or statute. It is the duty of the lower courts of the United States to abide by these previously-held decisions made in regards to federal constitutional law, with the United States Supreme Court serving as the ultimate authority in constitutional interpretation. Supreme Court constitutional interpretations hold ultimate authority in the United States; only the Supreme Court may overturn its previously-held decisions regarding the Constitution. As the Supreme Court passes judgment on matters of constitutional law, they set precedents that essentially become laws in themselves under the American legal concept of *stare decisis,* Latin for "to stand by that which is decided." This legal principle binds lower courts to the decisions made by the courts above them. Any court can set a precedent, although a conflicting ruling of a higher court will outweigh those of lower courts. While decisions made by one state's court system are not binding on another, they can be persuasive legal references. However, decisions made by the United States Supreme Court are binding on all states and lower courts. When two courts of equal footing set contradictory precedents, this is known as a "split" decision, and must thereafter be decided by the highest applicable court; in the case of constitutional questions, this is the Supreme Court of the United States.

> **Discussion:** *What is an example of a foreign country whose laws or lack of order cause its society to fall on one extreme of the totalitarian/anarchy continuum? What are the consequences for its citizens? What is an example of a country that falls on the opposite side of the continuum? In what ways do citizens in that country fare better or worse than citizens in the first country? What are the benefits of stare decisis for a representative democracy like the United States? How does this doctrine compliment the rule of law?*

The Fourth Amendment

Perhaps the Constitution's most important impact for private investigators is its effect on the federal privacy rights of U.S. citizens. The Fourth Amendment, which prohibits unreasonable **searches and seizures** of persons and property, is the source of most privacy rights in the United States. The Fourth Amendment reads in its entirety:

> *The right of the people to be secure in their persons, houses, papers, and effects, against unreasonable searches and seizures, shall not be violated, and no warrants shall issue, but upon probable cause, supported by oath or affirmation and particularly describing the place to be searched, and the persons or things to be searched.*

Although the word "privacy" is not found anywhere in the Fourth Amendment, it is well established that a right to privacy is implicit in its interpretation. Laws such as those regulating surreptitious phone recordings emanate from this implied right to privacy. While the amendment itself is only a short paragraph, a number of Supreme Court decisions have further defined it, and countless books have been written about these interpretations and how they have been applied to law and society.

The Fourth Amendment has been generally interpreted to contain two clauses, known as the *reasonableness clause* and the *warrant clause*. The warrant clause also has individual sub-requirements, such as the *particularity clause*, which requires those seeking search warrants to describe with specificity where they intend to search and what contraband they believe they will find. The distinction between the two major clauses is interpreted to mean that warrants are not required for all searches, provided first that they are *reasonable*. It is generally held that a search does not necessarily have to meet the evidentiary threshold of probable cause to be considered "reasonable", provided the search is not overly invasive. However, in cases where a warrant is required to conduct a search, it must meet the standards set forth in the warrant clause: probable cause must exist, the particularity clause must be met, and the requestor must swear under oath that the details listed in the affidavit are true and correct to the best of the affiant's knowledge. There are additional common law requirements related to warrants, such as that they must be reviewed by a fair and impartial person capable of determining probable cause (e.g., a magistrate or judge); they must be served in the daytime whenever possible; the person serving the warrant must announce his presence before entering the place to be searched; and once executed, the officer must prepare an inventory and return all of the seized items, etc.

A search is an examination of a person's body or belongings, or any other area where there is a reasonable expectation of privacy. Most searches—with few exceptions that are largely irrelevant to private investigators—require probable cause, and many searches also require a warrant. However, in areas where there is no reasonable expectation of privacy, there is no need to conduct a "search" under the legal definition of the word, therefore no probable cause or other level of evidence sufficiency is necessary. This includes when there is consent, or when an expectation of privacy has otherwise been waived, such as when a subject throws evidence in the trash, or when an employee agrees to his employer's search policy that allows the employer to review his email at any time. In these examples, the subjects have waived any claim to an expectation of privacy. Those areas are therefore open to scrutiny without the constitutional protections constraining legally defined searches. The latter example of waiving privacy rights is highly significant to private investigators who are often tasked with conducting investigations within workspaces, because privacy may be waived as a matter of employment and sometimes customer policy.

> *Discussion: From an employer's standpoint, what sound business practices might be instituted to place constraints on the degree that customers, employees, and vendors have a reasonable expectation of privacy in the workplace? How might these sound business practices make a subsequent investigation easier in the workplace?*

As a general rule, all searches performed by government agents require the issuance of a **search warrant**, except in certain broadly-defined exigency exceptions, such as the search of an automobile when probable cause exists, or property involved in what has been termed "hot pursuit"—when a law enforcement officer actively pursues a fleeing suspect into an area otherwise protected by a reasonable expectation of privacy. A warrant may only be obtained and executed by sworn law enforcement authorities, although information supplied by private investigators and other citizens may be used in affidavits to support a search warrant application. Law enforcement authorities routinely complete a sworn affidavit that details the basis for probable cause and describes the place and items to be searched. Information in the affidavit may be based on hearsay, and the affiant need not provide the names of any informants. However, the affiant generally must outline both the informant's basis of knowledge of the facts provided in the affidavit, and those factors indicative of the informant's veracity in providing those facts.

> *Discussion: Why are law enforcement authorities required to clearly establish an informant's basis of knowledge and truth in his or her statements? If this were not the rule, how might the government abuse the use of hearsay in the application for a warrant?*

Probable cause is defined as a reasonable basis of belief that a person has committed or is about to commit a crime, or that a place contains evidence relevant to a crime. Probable cause is an example of evidence sufficiency, also known as a *standard of proof*, which is the threshold of certainty that must be met for a procedure to occur in the legal process. Probable cause is the level of evidence sufficiency required for lawful arrest and questioning, and for searches and seizures. To bring this concept more clearly into focus, imagine a laboratory test tube being filled with a liquid, where the liquid represents evidence that an individual has committed or is about to commit a crime. Proof beyond a reasonable doubt sufficient for a criminal conviction would mean the test tube is filled nearly to the top. By comparison, the threshold for probable cause is approximately the point at which the tube is filled to twenty-five percent capacity. As a practical matter, probable cause is close to another standard of proof along the continuum known as *preponderance of the evidence*. Often coined "the greater weight of the evidence," preponderance of the evidence is the point at which the test tube is filled fifty-one percent to capacity in our example.

Prior to 1967, the courts held that the Fourth Amendment primarily protected individual property rights, not privacy rights, per se. This distinction changed after *Katz v. United States*.[25] The case involved a man, Katz, who was convicted in South Carolina federal court under an eight-count indictment charging him with transmitting wagering information by telephone from Los Angeles to Miami and Boston, thereby violating a federal criminal gambling statute. At trial, the government was permitted to introduce evidence of Katz's end of telephone conversations overheard by FBI agents who had attached an electronic listening and recording device to the outside of the public telephone booth where he placed his calls. The law had previously sanctioned eavesdropping from the *outside* of a physical dwelling or structure (e.g., a house, a phone booth, etc.) without a warrant, because the sanctity of the property or space was not violated. Accordingly, in affirming his conviction, the Ninth Circuit Court of Appeals rejected the contention that the recordings had been obtained in violation of the Fourth Amendment, because "[t]here was no physical entrance into the area occupied by [the petitioner]."[26] However, the Supreme Court reversed that decision, holding that the FBI's actions required a warrant, since Katz had a *reasonable expectation of privacy* while in the phone booth. [Since this landmark decision, the standard test to determine if property is considered protected under the Fourth Amendment is whether the underlying circumstances warrant both a subjective *and* objective expectation of privacy. In other words, an expectation of privacy exists if the subject of the action deems the circumstances private, and this expectation of privacy is reasonable given society's objective standards. For example, while placing fences and "no trespassing" signs on the perimeter of one's property increases the subjective expectation of privacy, society's objective standard, sometimes referred to as the "reasonable man" standard, maintains that signs and fences alone are not enough to afford one complete privacy from public view.] The standard used in *Katz* has carried over into areas other than constitutional law, such that intrusions into an area or situation where a subject has a "reasonable expectation of privacy" can expose even private investigators to common law tort actions such as invasion of privacy and intrusion into seclusion.

As a rule, only searches that fall under exigency and a few other exceptions do not require a search warrant. For law enforcement, these exceptions allow searches that are affected in hot pursuit of a suspect or that are conducted of automobiles without a warrant. Other exceptions also exist, such as searches incident to arrest, protective sweeps, and border searches. What constitutes a search depends on the degree of the reasonable expectation of privacy in that space. The greater the expectation of privacy in any particular area, the more likely a warrant will be required. For example, because people can generally expect a great deal of privacy in and around their homes, searches there almost always require a warrant, including the area surrounding someone's home, known as the home's "curtilage." The curtilage is roughly analogous to a suburban lawn. This means a private investigator is universally prohibited from entering a subject's home without expressed consent. An investigator should only enter the curtilage for purposes of knocking on the door or servicing legal process—not for conducting searches or surveillance. A similar reasonable expectation of privacy also exists inside cars; in people's clothing, handbags, and baggage; and in privately-owned offices and businesses, albeit less so in such areas' public spaces (e.g., in the lobby, elevators, and public corridors of office buildings, and the public shopping areas of grocery stores).

Outside these constitutionally protected areas, the public sphere is typically considered an **open field**, meaning there is little expectation of privacy with what occurs outside on the street, potentially within the view of others. This is true even on private property, regardless of how many fences there are, or whether the property is posted "no trespassing," provided the space is not within a property's private curtilage. This does not mean that private investigators can traverse private property in violation of trespassing or other laws, but it does mean that to examine or observe a space's "open field" is not, per se, a constitutionally defined search. As a practical matter, investigators working as agents of parties in court actions generally have less exposure to exclusion of evidence or tort liability when entering onto private property, even if the property is posted "no trespassing" or the owner of the property tells the investigator to stay away. However, the closer the area is to the protected curtilage, especially if the curtilage and the open field are divided by a fence, the more any investigation intending only *observation* is likely to invade the subject's reasonable expectation of privacy.

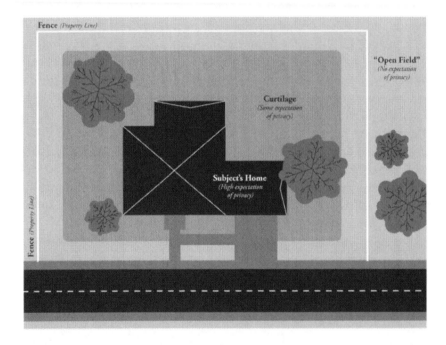

Areas outside a home's curtilage are not considered private, and almost always may be traveled with impunity. Areas within a home's curtilage are strictly off limits for purposes of searches and surveillance. For example, approaching the windows of a home and peering inside would clearly be an illegal invasion of privacy, whereas viewing a home from the street would be permissible.[27] It is okay to peer over the fence into a home's curtilage area (e.g., with a ladder), provided the investigator is not physically within the space. To illustrate by example, assume that a private investigator is tasked with investigating a subject who lives on a farm. Assume the entire farm is encircled by a barbed wire fence, and the subject's home is set back several hundred feet from the street or any other public property. The investigator is seeking to interview the subject and serve him a summons—in other words, not merely to *observe* the subject or conduct surveillance—so she may cross over the barbed wire fence and enter the home's curtilage to knock on the subject's door. In contrast, if the investigator was only conducting surveillance and crossed the barbed wire fence onto the subject's private property, she must remain a reasonably safe distance from the home and its curtilage at all times.

> ***Discussion:*** *Assume you have been tasked with conducting surveillance on a subject at your home or in the office building where you work. In what specific areas or "open fields" would you be permitted to observe the subject relative to that space? In the case of your home, where would lie the boundaries of the home's curtilage? In what areas of the office building would there be a high expectation of privacy? Could you conduct surveillance in those areas?*

Closely related to the concept of the "open field" doctrine is the Fourth Amendment concept of **plain view**, which conveys the idea that to plainly observe or otherwise perceive through the senses, such as touch and smell, something typically associated with the commission of a crime is not a constitutionally defined search. In the case of law enforcement, for example, to conduct a valid traffic stop and to subsequently observe a gun resting in plain view on the dashboard provides the officer with probable cause necessary for a search and possibly an arrest. The act of sensing the presence of the weapon does not constitute a search and therefore does not require probable cause. For the plain view doctrine to apply, however, the object must be immediately apparent to the senses without manipulation or any sensual enhancement. For example, if, in the previous example, the police officer, without probable cause, first moved a map that had been resting on the dashboard to uncover the theretofore unseen weapon, this would not have been plain view and would likely have been a constitutional violation (i.e., an illegal search). The plain view concept for probable cause also relates to all other senses of the human body: feeling a weapon through a suspect's clothes, smelling marijuana wafting out of a window, hearing the screams of a victim, etc. What is important to note for a private investigator is that she may observe anything that is within plain view, provided of course, that it is in an "open field" or that she is legitimately on the premises, but the simple act of moving an object a few inches where a reasonable expectation of privacy otherwise exists, so as to see what lies underneath, may constitute an invasion of privacy. For example, while conducting an interview of a witness at his home and gaining permission to use the restroom, it would be a privacy violation to then open the medicine cabinet and rummage for evidence. However, if a bottle of pills was resting in plain view on the wash basin, the investigator could legitimately write down the information contained on the prescription label.

Fifth Amendment

Another amendment of interest to private investigators is the Fifth Amendment, which covers many areas relevant to criminal procedure. The area of primary concern to private investigators involves the "self-incrimination clause." The Fifth Amendment reads in its entirety:

No person shall be held to answer for a capital, or otherwise infamous crime, unless on presentment or indictment of a grand jury, except in cases arising in the land or naval forces, or in the Militia, when in actual service in time of War or public danger; nor shall any person be subject for the same offense to be twice put in jeopardy of life or limb; nor shall be compelled in any criminal case to be a witness against himself, nor be deprived of life, liberty, or property, without due process of law; nor shall private property be taken for public use, without just compensation.

The self-incrimination clause only applies to testimonial evidence (not physical evidence) relevant to a criminal matter that might implicate the subject. It is important to note, however, that this constitutional protection only extends to the evidence received when the subject is *compelled* to provide information. The circumstances applicable to the Fifth Amendment are not limited to trial testimony. Any time a government agent seeks to compel a subject to provide information, such as during a custodial interview or interrogation, the Fifth Amendment will generally apply to any information that might later be used in a criminal proceeding against that person. This fact does not necessarily mean that agents are required to notice witnesses of their Fifth Amendment rights in every circumstance. For example, it is not necessary to inform a witness of his rights prior to him taking the stand, and, in fact, once a witness waives his Fifth Amendment protection and chooses to testify, he may be compelled to answer all questions. In other words, when taking the stand at trial, subjects cannot plead "the Fifth" on some subjects but not on others during cross-examination. Additionally, the protections are not extended to civil matters or to certain matters peripherally related to criminal justice where the goal is not punishment, but rather rehabilitation (e.g., civil commitment hearings).

The well-known **Miranda warnings** became part of the canon of Fifth Amendment law and were incorporated as standard law enforcement procedure in the Supreme Court's decision in *Miranda v. Arizona.*[28] The *Miranda* case initially began as four separate cases in which the defendants, while in police custody, were questioned by police officers, detectives, and a prosecuting attorney in a room in which they were cut off from the outside world. None of the defendants were given a full and effective warning of his rights at the onset of the interrogation process. In all four cases, the questioning elicited oral admissions, and, in three of them, signed statements that were admitted at trial. All the defendants were convicted. The Supreme Court found this to be a violation of the suspects' constitutional rights, and mandated that confessions would not be admissible as evidence at trial unless law enforcement and government agents, when conducting custodial interrogations (i.e., those in which the subject is officially considered a suspect and is in the official custody of law enforcement), provide an advisement of the right to assistance of counsel and protection against self-incrimination. Although the standard warnings have become part of our popular culture in countless film and television police dramas, the important points that the agent must address in each situation are that the subject has a right to remain silent; the things that he says to law enforcement can be used against him in a court of law; he has a right to an attorney; and he is entitled to be provided with an attorney if he cannot afford one.

Two factors trigger the requirement of a Miranda warning. First, the interview must be custodial—interpreted to mean that a reasonable person in the same situation would believe that he is not free to leave after a reasonably short amount of time. This standard also defines arrest. The second factor is that the person must be questioned as to his relationship to a crime, or in other words, as a suspect. For example, a person cannot invoke protection under the Fifth Amendment while being questioned by police about the activities of others. While these two factors may seem obvious, it is important to note that a subject who voluntarily speaks to the police while not in custody does not require a Miranda warning. Similarly, a subject who blurts out an admission before any questions are asked, even while in custody, cannot later claim that his Fifth Amendment rights were violated.

An **arrest** is the seizure or forcible restraint of a suspect. Only law enforcement authorities are permitted to make an arrest. The test for whether an arrest has occurred is typically construed as the point where a reasonable person would assume that he would not be free to leave after a reasonable amount of time, or where the seizure of the person is unreasonably invasive. An arrest does not have to be forcible; the force only need be implied. Therefore, it is imperative that a private investigator carefully address any indication that an interview subject expresses about being compelled to speak. While no Miranda warning is required of private investigators, implying physical force in any way, or suggesting that a subject is not free to leave at any time, is tantamount to an illegal arrest, thereby exposing the investigator to a civil claim or criminal charge of false imprisonment.

From a law enforcement standpoint, an arrest may either be legal, mistaken, or illegal. For police, it is a **mistaken arrest** if the basis for probable cause is later discovered to be unfounded due to no fault of the officer making the arrest. The distinction is important because the government is liable for **illegal arrests**, but not for mistaken arrests. For example, evidence obtained from legal searches caused by a mistaken arrest is still admissible in court, whereas the fruits of an illegal arrest will typically be excluded. Law enforcement may also not be sued for a mistaken arrest. However, no such standard exists for an arrest made by a private investigator or other private citizen. For private citizens (including private investigators) an arrest may only be legal or illegal. While citizen's arrests are allowable (i.e., a **legal arrest**) for felonies, provided the private citizen acted in good faith and probable cause existed for the seizure, citizens who choose to engage in such arrests can be held liable for any unreasonable mistakes in ways that law enforcement officers are not. If a citizen affects an arrest and it is later determined that no probable cause existed, or that an unreasonable amount of force was applied during the seizure, the arrest will be illegal and she will be liable for any number of tort actions, including battery and false imprisonment. It is therefore *strongly* advised that a private investigator never engages in a citizen's arrest, save in bona fide emergencies.

> **Discussion:** *What factors could be used to establish voluntariness? What factors might suggest to a reasonable person that he is not free to leave during an investigation? Are there any sound business practices that a private investigator should adhere to that would prevent allegations of an illegal arrest?*

19

Important Legal Concepts

Evidence

Evidence is any document, testimony, or tangible object that may prove or disprove an alleged fact of a case in a court of law. Evidence ranges from an affidavit signed by a witness in a harassment investigation to DNA obtained from a bloody footprint left at a murder scene. The *raison d'être* of a private investigator is to gather evidence; every witness an investigator interviews and every object or document that she reviews is potential evidence in a subsequent proceeding. Since it is impossible to know what evidence will be important at the time a fact or object is observed during an investigation, it is imperative that all evidence be treated as if it were critical to the case. The **rules of evidence** are exceedingly complicated, and there are many nuances and exceptions to what will or will not be deemed admissible. Generally, evidence must be deemed competent, material, and relevant before it is admissible in court or at a deposition. There are also a myriad of other rules concerning hearsay, the admission of scientific evidence, the exclusion of evidence obtained in violation of constitutional limitations, and the right of cross-examination.

Evidence is deemed to be incompetent when its veracity is suspect, or when it is unfairly prejudicial or based on hearsay. The competency of evidence is the factor most controllable by an investigator, since she often will be the first to gather and secure the evidence. Asking leading questions during an interview, storing real evidence in a haphazard manner, and showing bias during an investigation are all likely to influence a judge's decision as to whether the evidence in question is **competent** and therefore admissible. It is imperative that an investigator refrain from partisanship or other bias, and take great care in the manner by which she elicits information or secures and stores evidence during an investigation. The proper methods for collecting and storing evidence are detailed in Part III of this textbook.

The next test, after competence is established, is whether evidence is **material** and **relevant** to the issue in question. Materiality and relevance are closely related but distinct concepts. Evidence is material when it is related logically to a legal or factual issue presented during a case, while relevant evidence tends to prove or disprove a consequential matter at issue. Unlike with relevance, material evidence need not necessarily prove or disprove a particular fact in question; it must only relate logically in some manner. Whether material evidence is admitted depends to a large extent on what it is intended to prove or show. It follows that material evidence is not necessarily relevant, but relevant evidence is necessarily material. Material evidence is routinely admitted when it is not relevant, as the issue of relevance is often somewhat subjective and contentious.

Beyond the issue of admissibility, evidence is typically classified as being either real, testimonial, or demonstrative. Additionally, evidence can be either direct or circumstantial. The two classifications of evidence are inclusive of the other, such that evidence, for example, can be both testimonial and direct, or real and circumstantial. The only general correlation is that direct evidence tends to be testimonial, because real or demonstrative evidence cannot "speak" directly to the facts of a case without the explanation provided by another source, such as an expert. **Direct evidence** must be based on personal observation or knowledge, and, if competent, proves a fact without inference. Conversely, **circumstantial evidence** is solely based on inference and lacks personal knowledge. Direct evidence will almost always be testimonial, because it takes an actual person to have "personal knowledge" or to personally observe something. All evidence that is not direct is necessarily circumstantial. Although direct evidence is generally considered the more powerful of the two forms of evidence, cases built solely upon direct evidence tend to be weak, because the witnesses in these cases are sometimes susceptible to impeachment.

The next group of classification includes **testimonial evidence**, which is when a witness takes the stand and testifies under oath as to what he witnessed or otherwise sensed. In very limited cases, testimonial evidence may be presented in the form of a sworn statement, audio recording, or deposition if the witness is unavailable at trial. However, in most cases the witness must take the stand, testify under penalty of perjury, and be subject to cross-examination. Much of the evidence dealt with during private investigations is testimonial. While the facts relayed during an interview (or written statements) are not considered testimonial evidence, per se, they are valuable insofar as they determine the likely facts that will come out during the subsequent testimony, and—should the witness later alter those facts from what was earlier told to the investigator—he may be impeached on the stand for making previous statements inconsistent with his sworn testimony. An investigator need not necessarily obtain a sworn statement or affidavit for the facts to later be brought up at trial, but having a written account generally buttresses an investigator's testimony, should the facts ever come into question.

Next, **real evidence** is anything physical that is material to the facts at issue. It may include documents, emails, blood specimens, surveillance tapes—i.e., anything tangible or "real." Such evidence may include video surveillance footage obtained by an investigator, or the investigator's reports generated during an investigation. When these objects are admitted into evidence, presumably because they are material and relevant to the facts at issue and are not covered by legal privilege, they become real evidence that may influence the case. It is therefore important that investigators remain cognizant of the manner by which they collect and preserve evidence during an investigation, and how they have the potential to generate new evidence during an investigation.

When the interpretation of the relevance of real evidence hinges upon the testimony of an expert witness, its admissibility is determined by several factors intended to establish the scientific validity of the witness's field of expertise. In the federal court system, these factors are sometimes referred to as *Daubert* questions after the case that determined the standards,[29] although the rules were later clarified in the Federal Rules of Evidence.[30] The issues affecting whether the testimony will be admissible include: whether the underlying theory or technique has been tested and subjected to peer review; whether the error rate for the technique is known or quantifiable; whether there are standards of control to mitigate the potential for errors; and the extent to which the technique has been accepted in the scientific community. The last factor, general scientific acceptability—sometimes referred to as the *Frye* test[31]—was the test that applied in federal court prior to the revision of the federal rules in 1975.[32]

Finally, **demonstrative evidence** is that which is not "real" in the sense that it is not directly related to or derived from the incident at issue; rather, demonstrative evidence is created or obtained by one party in a case to demonstrate an element of that case. A map, satellite image, or photograph taken to demonstrate a crime scene are examples of demonstrative evidence. This type of evidence, typically created well after the underlying incident has occurred, is used to demonstrate some broad fact, such as the fact that an area was dimly lit or that two stationary objects are a particular distance apart.

Other important evidentiary concepts include the **hearsay rules and exceptions**. Hearsay is evidence—typically testimonial evidence—that is submitted secondhand and not from its original source. Hearsay is generally excluded in a court of law, but there are exceptions. These exceptions include excited utterances, contemporaneously recorded recollections, and admissions of guilt such as those obtained during an interrogation. Also, prior inconsistent statements are admissible for purposes of impeachment, even though they are technically hearsay. Other hearsay exceptions include the admission of official records, prior testimony, and statements made to medical personnel.

An investigator obtaining a sworn statement from a witness may increase the likelihood that parts of the statement will be exceptions to the hearsay rules by including observations of tangible characteristics in the document. For example, if during the interview, the witness states that his co-worker appeared "angry" about not receiving a promotion, the investigator should ask the witness to identify his firsthand observations that support his conclusion that the co-worker was angry. Such observable factors might include that the co-worker was speaking in a "loud voice," had a "red face," used "erratic hand gestures," etc. While the actual *words* used may or may not be admissible into evidence under hearsay rules, the witness's firsthand observations of his co-worker's mannerisms will almost definitely come into evidence, provided they meet other evidentiary requirements. Also, investigators gathering official documentary evidence from courts and government agencies can increase the likelihood that the evidence will later be admissible by having the documents officially certified or true-tested. This typically involves having the court or agency emboss or stamp the documents with their official seal. In other cases, the investigator may have the custodian of records for the government agency or private business complete an affidavit certifying that the documents are authentic copies of official documents produced in the normal course of business.

Another important evidentiary rule that only applies to state actors is termed the **exclusionary rule**. This rule requires the suppression of evidence obtained in violation of a criminal defendant's constitutional rights, and also includes the exclusion of any evidence derived from unconstitutional searches. The exclusionary rule was established in the federal courts after the case of *Weeks v. United States*,[33] but the rule was not applied to state court cases until years later.[34] In the *Weeks* case, the defendant's house was searched without a warrant and he was arrested for using the mail service to transport illegal lottery tickets. He was initially convicted in a trial court, but the U.S. Supreme Court reversed the verdict, ruling that the evidence against him should have been excluded at trial. In a later case, federal agents conducted an illegal search of a business while the owners were in police custody. In an effort to circumvent the exclusionary rule, the police made copies of the evidence and then returned it to the business before issuing subpoenas for return of the evidence to the court. When the defendants would not comply with the subpoenas, they were convicted of contempt of court. In reversing the trial court decision in this case, the Supreme Court found that not only illegally-obtained evidence must be excluded from trial, but any evidence derived from illegal searches and seizures must be excluded from evidence. This rule is often referred to as the "fruits of the poisonous tree" doctrine.[35]

The exclusionary rule and the fruits of the poisonous tree doctrine only apply to law enforcement agents—not to private investigators, unless the investigator is deemed a state actor. There are many exceptions to these evidentiary rules. For example, evidence may be admissible for purposes of impeaching a witness, irrespective of whether it was obtained constitutionally or not. The exclusionary rule does not apply to evidence presented in non-criminal matters, such as immigration hearings, or in non-trial venues for criminal cases, such as grand jury proceedings and parole hearings.

There are also important federal rules regarding **exculpatory evidence**. Evidence that is exculpatory tends to establish the innocence of criminal defendants. The opposite of exculpatory is inculpatory, which is evidence that tends to establish guilt. In federal criminal cases, the prosecution is required to disclose to the defense all evidence requested that is material to guilt or punishment, including exculpatory evidence. This is sometimes referred to as ***Brady* evidence**, after the applicable case law.[36] *Brady* evidence also includes agreements between federal prosecutors and cooperating witnesses not to seek prosecution in return for testimony (i.e., plea bargains). This evidence is referred to as **_Giglio_ evidence**.[37] From the standpoint of private investigators working for the defense in federal criminal prosecutions, _Brady_ and _Giglio_ evidence provide a significant advantage. There is nothing analogous to these rules regarding exculpatory evidence in the Virginia court system, meaning that criminal defendants are provided very little information from the prosecution about the evidence related to their charges.

Another important federal evidentiary rule applies to what is known as **_Jencks_ evidence**.[38] This rule provides that parties in federal criminal cases are entitled to discover any written statements pertaining to an adversarial witness that are related to that witness's testimony. _Jencks_ material that must be provided by the defendant to the prosecutor is sometimes referred to as _"reverse Jencks."_ Investigators conducting investigations for federal criminal matters must be aware that any substantially verbatim or otherwise contemporaneously recorded statement obtained from a cooperative witness may be discoverable by the opposition. This discoverable evidence includes grand jury transcripts, written and audio statements, and sometimes even an investigator's notes, depending on when they were taken and their level of detail. The general rule to follow when conducting federal criminal defense investigations is to refrain from taking significant notes or sworn statements from defense witnesses, as such documentary evidence may be discoverable when these witnesses take the stand. However, there is no disadvantage to taking notes or statements from government witnesses, as these witnesses will only be called to testify for the opposition, meaning the evidence will not be discoverable. Neither the prosecutor nor the defense attorney need actually disclose statements pursuant to _Jencks_ until the witness testifies.[39] Similar to _Brady_ and _Giglio_ evidence, _Jencks_ does not apply in Virginia state courts, so any notes or statements obtained from interviews with witnesses in criminal cases will not be discoverable by the opposition. Therefore, in Virginia, there is no legal reason for investigators not to take sworn statements from every witness or make audio recordings of every interview.

> **_Discussion:_** _Provide examples of direct and circumstantial evidence. Is direct evidence always better than circumstantial evidence? What is an example of a very compelling and relevant piece of circumstantial evidence? Assume you are working for a criminal defendant charged with a crime in federal court and you are concerned about creating discoverable Jencks material. How would you gauge whether to obtain a sworn statement_

from a witness? Why would you be concerned about creating evidence that is discoverable by the opposition?

State and Federal Courts

The two functionally autonomous court systems in the United States are federal courts and state courts. The federal court system is comprised of a number of federal jurisdictions, but, unlike state courts, no distinction is drawn between courts of limited and general jurisdiction; that is, most federal trial courts are simply called district courts, not to be confused with the district courts that make up the courts of limited jurisdiction in some state court systems. This is significant because novice investigators sometimes confuse, for example, the Alexandria General District Court with the U.S. District Court for the Eastern District of Virginia, which happens to have a court located in Alexandria, Virginia. There are also relatively autonomous federal trial courts that address specific issues of federal law, namely the Court of International Trade, the Court of Federal Claims, and federal bankruptcy courts operating as a separate branch of each federal district court. Federal courts only have jurisdiction over cases involving questions of federal law, including issues related to the U.S. Constitution, and cases in which there are legal disputes between citizens of different states. In contrast, the state courts are concerned with, and authorized to exercise jurisdiction over, matters of both state and federal common law. Rulings by the U.S. Supreme Court are the ultimate authority regarding all matters of federal and constitutional law, and rulings by the state supreme courts are the final authority over any matter related to their respective state laws.

Within each state court system, there are courts of limited jurisdiction, courts of general jurisdiction, and appellate courts. Almost all courts decide both civil and criminal matters. The hierarchical structure for each state court system, beginning at the bottom, includes the courts of limited jurisdiction, in Virginia called general district courts; followed by the courts of general jurisdiction, in Virginia called circuit courts; followed by the state's appellate courts which hear appeals of general court decisions. The highest level of the typical state court system is the court of final decision, often named the supreme court of that state. The state court of final decision does exactly that—makes the most final, binding decisions on issues of law within that state. The courts of limited and general jurisdiction have different names in different states. For example, courts of general jurisdiction in New York are called supreme courts, while in California they are called superior courts.

Citizens have the most contact with the courts of limited jurisdiction, regarding, for example, most minor civil matters, traffic violations, misdemeanor criminal matters, and the preliminary hearings held for felony criminal matters. In comparison, courts of general jurisdiction are the courts with the broadest powers, where most major cases of civil and felony criminal matters are tried.

Except for the court of final decision (often named the supreme court), state court systems are generally divided by counties or districts. In Virginia, for example, there are thirty-two courts of limited jurisdiction, also known as general district courts. In terms of civil law, these courts are where plaintiffs, upon filing a complaint or civil warrant with the court clerk and paying a nominal fee, initiate most civil claims of less than $15,000.[40] Each city and county in the Commonwealth has a designated general district court, where judges—elected to sit on the bench for six-year terms—hear all civil and criminal trials. In other words, there are no jury trials in general district courts in Virginia. Misdemeanor cases that have been appealed from a general district court to a circuit court following a verdict in favor of the government are tried in circuit court *de novo* before a jury. This means that the evidence is essentially presented all over again, this time with a jury instead of a judge to weigh the facts.[41] For criminal matters, misdemeanors are tried in general district courts in Virginia. A **misdemeanor** is any charge that carries a penalty less than one year in jail or a fine of up to $2,500, or both. In contrast, a **felony** is any crime punishable by more than one year of incarceration and up to the ultimate penalty—death. The maximum sentence in a misdemeanor is sometimes semantically referred to in sentencing as "twelve months," as opposed to "one year." Persons found guilty of misdemeanors in Virginia will complete half their sentence, minus any time off for good behavior, while those convicted of felonies will serve eighty percent of their sentence. There is no parole in Virginia. Typical misdemeanors include simple assault, theft, trespassing, prostitution, and minor vandalism. The district courts also hold **preliminary hearings** in felony criminal matters to determine whether there is probable cause to justify holding the defendant for a grand jury hearing.

Virginia's circuit courts are its courts of general jurisdiction and are divided into thirty-one judicial circuits with 120 separate circuit courts in the various counties and cities. Interestingly, in the state of Virginia,

there are thirty-two judicial districts but only thirty-one judicial circuits.[42] The discrepancy is due to the 2nd Judicial Circuit, which includes
both Virginia Beach and the Eastern Shore, meaning that two judicial
districts are represented by a single judicial circuit.[43] Generally, one circuit court is assigned to each county and independent city, which means
that Virginia should have 134 circuits, one for each of the ninety-five
individual counties and thirty-four independent cities. But the number
of circuit courts is actually 120, because there are some independent
cities that share a court with adjacent jurisdictions.

Circuit courts are the trial courts with the broadest powers in Virginia. Judges, elected to sit on the bench for eight-year terms, hear most
civil cases with claims exceeding $15,000, and all felonies and family
matters including divorce cases. Circuit courts also have jurisdiction over
the trial of misdemeanors originally charged in circuit court, and all
criminal and civil cases appealed from district court.

FEDERAL AND STATE
TRIALS AND APPELATE COURTS

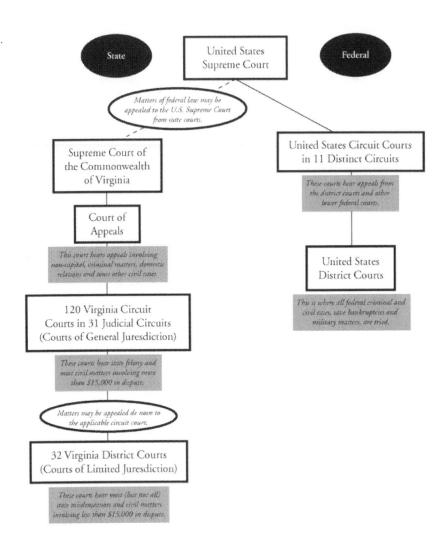

Most criminal matters heard in circuit courts are felonies. After what are known as the *bind over* decisions are made by judges in felony preliminary hearings held at district court, a grand jury determines whether the defendant will be indicted and held for trial by the circuit court. An **indictment**, also known as a true bill, is the formal accusation of a felony made by a grand jury and presented to the circuit court for prosecution against the defendant. No defendant may be prosecuted for a felony in Virginia without return of a true bill from a paneled grand jury. A regular **grand jury** is composed of five to seven citizens of the jurisdiction where the circuit court is located, sitting for at least six-month stints. Grand jury proceedings are held *ex parte*, meaning the grand jury members are only presented with the government's side of the case. Its mission is to establish the basis for probable cause, not to determine the guilt or innocence of the defendant (which is done later by a petit jury). In addition to regular grand juries, there are also *special* grand juries, which are comprised of seven to eleven citizens tasked with proactively investigating criminal activity, often at the recommendation of the members of a regular grand jury, when the information provided by the government suggests other conditions that beg further investigation.[44] It is important to note, however, that a criminal indictment is not a constitutional guarantee because the U.S. Supreme Court has stated that it is not a "fundamental right."[45] Therefore, criminal statutes in some states may allow what is called a prosecutorial information, thereby foregoing the grand jury process and bringing forth the charges without an indictment. In some states, including Virginia, a defendant who has yet to be indicted but chooses to plead guilty to a crime may sometimes waive his right to a true bill and instead agree to the facts stipulated in a prosecutorial information.

Most cases are settled prior to trial. A settlement in criminal matters is referred to as a plea, plea deal, or plea bargain. Sometimes criminal defendants will plead *nolo contendere* or "no contest." A no contest plea is essentially a guilty plea where the defendant wishes to avoid automatic civil liability in a subsequent civil proceeding. There are also Alford pleas, which are tantamount to guilty pleas to be used for purposes of impeachment, employment, etc. An Alford plea differs from a simple guilty plea because a defendant is not necessarily admitting guilt, but only implicitly admitting that, had the case proceeded to trial, he would have been found guilty. In civil cases, settlements are usually monetary, although they may include other agreements. In some civil cases, settlement agreements are sealed and not available to the public.

Discussion: What is the purpose of a nolo contendere plea if it is essentially the same as a guilty plea? Besides guilt beyond a reasonable doubt and a preponderance of the evidence, what are other examples of evidentiary sufficiency in the legal system? Rank them from the lowest level of evidentiary sufficiency to the highest. Keeping in mind that federal and state jurisdictions are relatively autonomous from each other but otherwise overlap geographically, where might a defendant be charged with a murder that occurred in Alexandria, Virginia?

Trials

Cases that cannot be settled must be decided at trial. Trials typically consist of arguing legal motions and pleadings; the process of *voir dire*, whereby a jury is selected in jury trials; opening statements by the plaintiff's attorney and then the defendant's attorney; testimony of witnesses and presentation of evidence, beginning with the plaintiff's attorney and consisting of direct examination, cross-examination, and then re-direct, and sometimes re-cross; selection and presentation of jury instructions; closing arguments; and jury deliberations. This process oftentimes caps months and even years of legal procedure, typically involving discovery of evidence and other relevant documents and witness depositions. Because this process if often exceedingly expensive, the vast majority of cases, both criminal and civil, will never make it to trial before they are ultimately settled by agreement of the parties.

All criminal defendants are entitled to a **jury trial**; this is a constitutional guarantee. However, jury trials are rare in misdemeanor cases. Recall, for example, that jury trials only occur in circuit courts in Virginia. This is constitutional, because cases that have been appealed to circuit court after a verdict in favor of the government are tried in circuit court *de novo* before a jury. Trials before a judge are sometimes referred to as **bench trials**. Misdemeanor trials that have been successfully appealed from district court, or that are otherwise being tried in circuit court, have juries consisting of seven members. Felony defendants are automatically entitled to trials consisting of twelve jurors. In civil jury trials, cases involving $15,000 or less generally have five jurors, although civil matters involving more than $10,000 may have seven members, depending on the type of case.[46]

The legal process begins with the filing of a complaint and then involves what is known as **discovery**, where each party is required to provide information and evidence to the other party relevant to the dispute. A complaint or civil warrant is an example of a **pleading**, which is, generally speaking, a formal document where one party in the case sets forth or responds to allegations, claims, denials, or defenses. In the complaint, the plaintiff details the allegations and describes each alleged legal violation. In felonies, the indictment or information acts as the complaint in a criminal case. In civil cases, the complaint initiates the lawsuit and sets forth the argument for venue, the relevant allegations of fact, and a prayer for relief which specifies alleged damages. The defendant will then respond to the complaint by filing an answer, also a type of pleading, which specifically addresses the accusations laid out in the complaint either by admitting to them, outright denying them, or denying knowledge. Another example of a pleading is a demurrer, which is a response to a complaint filed by the defendant that challenges the allegations on some legal ground, essentially stating that, even if all the facts alleged in the complaint are true, the plaintiff still has no legal action to the recovery demanded.

After the complaint and the answer have been filed, the legal issues of a case, including the issuance of discovery, are argued through filing various **motions**. A motion is a written or oral application requesting a court to make a particular ruling or order. It can essentially be thought of as a request to a judge for a particular decision. A motion is usually a written document, but it may also be argued verbally before a judge. Types of motions include motions to dismiss the case on some procedural ground, for example, because a claim was filed after the statute of limitations; motions *in limine*; motions to compel; and motions for summary judgment. A motion *in limine* is a request that certain evidence not be presented or weighed at trial, typically because its admission would violate a rule of evidence. A motion to compel is a request for the judge to force or compel the other party to perform some action, such as to disclose particular evidence during discovery. Such a motion can additionally ask for sanctions, such as an award of attorney's fees, against the opposing party. A motion for summary judgment is made by either party in a civil matter after the discovery process has ended but before the trial. It is a motion that requests the judge to rule in favor of the moving party by granting relief or dismissing the case outright, typically arguing that the case cannot be decided otherwise in light of the available evidence. Motions for summary judgment are very important, because they help separate frivolous lawsuits or defenses from those that have merit. Cases are often settled after judges rule on a motion for summary judgment.

In civil matters, the discovery process also includes taking **depositions**, which involves witnesses being called to testify under oath, usually by the attorney of the opposing party. In depositions, the testimony is typically recorded, either by audio, video, or stenographer for purpose of gathering facts in preparation for trial. The testimony occurs substantially like regular trial testimony (but without a judge or a jury), with the deposing party engaging in direct questioning, followed by cross-examination by the non-deposing attorney, and then re-direct. Both sides may object frequently to questions asked during a deposition, but typically (with a few exceptions, such as those involving privilege) a deponent will be required to answer questions during the deposition; the objections will be preserved until trial.

Cases that make it to trial before a judge or jury are factually decided upon the applicable level of **evidentiary sufficiency,** also called standard of proof. The level of evidentiary sufficiency for all criminal cases is guilt beyond a reasonable doubt, with the burden of proof falling on the government. In many types of civil cases, the burden of proof shifts from the plaintiff to the defendant at different times during the process leading up to trial. However, the proof required for most civil matters is the preponderance of the evidence, generally defined as the greater weight of the evidence, or more than fifty percent certainty that a proposition is true. This is a much lower standard than that required for criminal convictions. Using the earlier example of a test tube filled with varying amounts of liquid, *guilt beyond a reasonable doubt* occurs when the test tube is approximately ninety-five percent full. Higher than *preponderance of the evidence*, but lower than *proof beyond a reasonable doubt*, the standard of *clear and convincing evidence* is required in certain civil cases, such as in civil commitment hearings and civil fraud cases. Clear and convincing evidence requires a proposition to be highly probable or reasonably certain. It is easiest to think of clear and convincing evidence as the point at which the figurative test tube is approximately seventy-five percent full.

EVIDENCE SUFFICIENCY

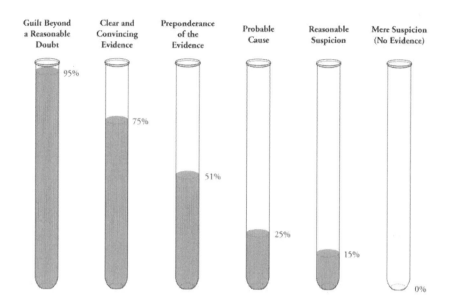

Trials are initiated with opening statements, and are decided by the presentment of evidence by both parties. Typically plaintiffs present their evidence first, followed by defendants. Each side presenting evidence first elicits their evidence from witnesses who take the stand under oath and penalty of perjury during direct questioning, and then the opposition is allowed to challenge that evidence during cross-examination. The side which initially presented the evidence then has an opportunity to clarify the testimonial evidence during re-direct questioning of their witness, followed by re-cross in some cases. After the presentment of all evidence, both sides present their closing arguments, which are intended to summarize the evidence in a manner that emphasizes the merits of their respective positions. It is important to realize that opening statements and closing arguments are not considered admissible evidence, and therefore may not be considered by judges and juries to decide the outcome of the case. Similarly, questions asked to elicit testimony from a witness on the stand are not evidence either. Only the presented evidence is admissible, although sometimes both parties may stipulate on some fact, which is then incorporated into evidence without it necessarily being presented.

After closing arguments, the judge or jury deliberates and reaches a **verdict**, or a ruling that encapsulates the findings of the trial. Even in jury trials, judges always decide matters of law; juries decide only matters of fact, guided by carefully constructed jury instructions which provide a roadmap to jurors, untrained in law, regarding how the facts of the case should be weighed according to the applicable laws. In bench trials, judges decide matters of law and fact. As a general rule, the facts of a case may not be overturned on appeal unless clearly in error. This makes the decisions of juries, for example, who were present to hear the testimony and better positioned than the appellate court to evaluate witness credibility, often immutable.

The decisions on matters of law are contestable through a process known as an **appeal**. In the event that a higher court finds that a judge erred on a critical matter of law during a trial, then the case may be remanded back to the trial court for retrial or dismissal. In Virginia, the final decision of the circuit court may be appealed to either the Supreme Court or the Court of Appeals, depending upon the type of case involved. Death penalty, lawyer disbarment, and many civil cases are appealed directly to the Supreme Court, while domestic relations cases and non-capital criminal cases tried in circuit courts are appealed to the Court of Appeals.[47]

> *Discussion:* Consider the alleged sexual assault involving David and Michelle from Chapter 11. What are the individual stages that will occur throughout the entire legal process, assuming the case goes to trial and is later appealed? Now imagine a civil claim for divorce. Assuming the case goes to trial and is appealed, list the stages that will occur from the start of the case to its conclusion.

Jurisdiction and Service of Process

Inextricably tied to the process of litigation is the **service of process**, which is the delivery of a summons, subpoena, or legal document to a party, witness, or person having relevant documentary or other physical evidence in a legal action. Before the court may exercise jurisdiction over a person or business, there must be the issuance and service of a legal document, typically a summons or subpoena, to that entity. How service of process must be affected depends on the legal requirements of service in the state or jurisdiction where the document is issued; if the entity to be served is a person or business; and whether that entity exists exclusively outside the jurisdiction of the court action. Generally, states have the exclusive right to determine the rules of service for their own citizens and for businesses residing within their borders.

The rules of services are more complicated, however, when the party to be served is extra-jurisdictional, when its whereabouts are unknown, or when it only holds property or other assets—but is otherwise not physically present—within the state's jurisdiction. The main issue in these instances is whether the underlying basis for a court proceeding is *in personam* or *in rem*.[48] An *in personam* proceeding is one intended solely to determine one's personal rights and obligations, while a proceeding *in rem* is intended to establish the personal status of the plaintiff vis-à-vis property or some other asset that is first seized by the state. Service to an out-of-state entity that is *in personam* must always be via personal service, which is one reason why states universally require businesses operating within their jurisdictions to have registered agents designated to accept legal process.[49] Service for an *in rem* proceeding may typically, but not always, be made via public notice in a newspaper, posting it on the door of the property in question, or via some other non-personal means proscribed by the state's statute. This only applies to extra-jurisdictional service; states determine the rules of service for both *in personam* and *in rem* cases when both parties reside within its jurisdiction.

The rules for a given jurisdiction typically hinge upon the type of legal document that is being served. A **subpoena** is a directive by a court for a subject to appear for testimony or for production of certain evidence. A subpoena necessarily requires *in personam* services, since ignoring a subpoena is cause for what is sometimes referred to as the attachment of the body, meaning that marshals or sheriffs may physically arrest the subject and bring him before the court pursuant to the service. A **summons**, on the other hand, is a document that notifies a defendant that he must appear before the court to answer a complaint filed by a plaintiff. In most cases, the summons is served to the defendant with the pleading attached. Whether a summons is *in personam* or *in rem* depends on the underlying legal action. There are also procedural requirements for the service of notice regarding motions and the like, although such service may typically be via regular mail or even facsimile. Virginia allows no service of civil process on Sunday.[50]

For a subpoena *duces tecum*, which loosely translates to, "bring it with you," the issuing party describes on the subpoena the documents, tangible objects, or electronic evidence that must be produced. A subpoena *duces tecum* does not require its recipient to produce a document that he does not have in his possession or that he would have to create or compile from other source documents. Subpoenas that are unreasonable or do not conform to the law may be quashed (invalidated) on a motion to the court. In Virginia, subpoenas may only be issued by judges, magistrates, court clerks, and the Commonwealth Attorney's Office.[51] Private attorneys obtain a subpoena by requesting the court to issue it. They may then opt to have the subpoena served by the sheriff or by a private citizen. In federal court, subpoenas may be issued directly by a private attorney representing a party in an action before the court, and must be accompanied by a $40 witness fee plus an estimated mileage allowance based upon the distance from the witness's location to the courthouse, multiplied by the prevailing reimbursable federal mileage rate. Federal subpoenas may be served within one hundred miles from the issuing court, and subpoenas issued by the Superior Court of the District of Columbia may be served within twenty-five miles of the city's borders, an area that encompasses several counties in Virginia and Maryland. Most state subpoenas may only be served within their own state's borders. When a subpoena must be served outside its jurisdiction, the issuing attorney must employ *letters rogatory* to request the jurisdiction where the subpoena will be served to open a miscellaneous court action so that a local subpoena may be issued to obtain jurisdiction over the subject through the convening court. *Letters rogatory* is also the process for serving subpoenas in foreign countries that are outside the normal reach of U.S. courts.

Subpoenas must generally be served by personal service, sometimes called hand delivery, in order for attachment of the body to apply. This means the process server must be in the subject's presence when the document is served, though it need not involve physically handing the subpoena to the subject. It only needs to be personal in the sense that the subject is aware he is being served and the investigator is within a close proximity to him. For example, in the event that a subject "refuses" to accept service, it is sufficient personal service for the investigator to simply inform the subject that he has been served and to place the subpoena on the ground or some other, suitable object, such as a desk or car windshield. Similarly, in the event that a subject refuses to open his door to accept process, but has otherwise identified himself, it would be valid personal service if the investigator left the subpoena in the door jamb.

Unlike a subpoena, a summons need not necessarily be served via *in personam* service. A summons may be served outside the jurisdiction where it was issued according to the rules of service for where it will be served. In other words, a summons issued by a Virginia court served in Boston must be served according to the rules of service in Massachusetts. A summons is the document that notifies the defendant that he is being sued, and is usually accompanied by the complaint. Both the summons and the complaint must be served to the defendant to establish the court's jurisdiction over that party. In the event that a defendant who has been served with a summons and a pleading does not file an answer or a demurrer, the court may issue a default judgment in favor of the plaintiff. Therefore, once served, defendants are normally highly motivated to respond within the time allotted. Although personal service of the defendant is preferable, service of a summons in Virginia and in many other states may be completed by leaving a copy of the paperwork with a family member over the age of sixteen who lives at the home, or—in the event that the process server is unsuccessful finding either the defendant or a suitable family member after a reasonably diligent effort—by mailing and posting a copy on the subject's door at least ten days before a possible judgment by default.[52]

If the defendant or recipient of a subpoena *duces tecum* is a company, service may be made by serving any officer or director of that company, or its registered agent.[53] An investigator may identify the registered agent of a company by contacting the state agency that licenses businesses in that jurisdiction. In Virginia, this is the State Corporation Commission. For cases that include defendants who are officers of companies and who are also named in a lawsuit both as individuals (e.g., individual officers of the company) and in their capacity as registered agents of the company, the summons and complaint must be served to each party properly (e.g., to each named individual and to the registered agent of the company). It is not acceptable, for example, to serve a summons to the family member of the president of a company in the same manner that the president might be served as an individual defendant.

In Virginia, any person over eighteen years of age who is not a party in the case may serve legal process. Although the terms "officer" and "sheriff" are sometimes found on the returns of subpoenas and summonses, these terms are used ambiguously to refer to the server of such process.[54] Serving process does not necessarily require that one have a private investigator license or registration, per se, although any investigation pursuant to an underlying court action, including efforts to locate the whereabouts of witnesses to be served with legal process, does require both a license and registration.

Because subjects rarely like to be served with process, it is logical that an investigator will want to correctly perform service on the first attempt. Investigators should assume, absent specific evidence to the contrary, that the subject will *not* dodge during the first attempt at service. In this manner, by treating a subject as if he will behave like a responsible citizen, he will usually act in kind and not avoid the investigator. However, there are plenty of exceptions. Many subjects will avoid service at all costs. Therefore, it is prudent to ask the client at the onset whether the subject knows that the service is forthcoming and how he is expected to react. Subjects who dodge service are best served with guile and patience. While sometimes it works for an investigator to pretend that she has a package for the subject at his home or work, this will almost never work for a subject who knows that someone is trying to serve him. It is therefore preferable to wait a couple blocks from the subject's home and serve him when he is out in the open and cannot use doors, family members, or receptionists to block for him. Having a photograph of the subject helps with this approach.

The service of all legal process requires that process server to file a return or affidavit of service with the court after valid service is conducted. The return is typically located on the reverse side of the subpoena or summons, although sometimes it is on the footer of the document itself. Because of this requirement, it is important for an investigator to maintain copies of the documents and information she needs to complete the affidavit and, once the service is completed, to note the exact date, time, manner (e.g., personal, domiciliary, etc.) of the service, and a brief physical description of the subject served.

Types of Civil Parties and Corporate Structures

When discussing trials and legal actions, it is important to understand the structure of legal entities. Lawsuits often involve companies, and deciding which parties are liable for the actions of a company is key to any investigation. Company structures can sometimes be very complicated, with one corporation controlling several subsidiaries that control other subsidiaries in a complicated pyramid. Knowing how companies function and understanding their legal limitations can provide clues as to how they are structured. In the United States, companies are filed at the state level, and are referred to as a "domestic" entity in the state where they were initially filed. The state where a company files as a domestic entity need not necessarily be where it is physically located. For example, it was once popular for companies to file in Delaware, where there were tax benefits for doing so, even though many of the officers of these companies had never set foot in the state. If a company also conducts business in another state, they must file as a "foreign" entity in that jurisdiction. Companies acting under a name different than the name of the owner must file a D/B/A, which stands for "doing business as," with the state government. This is also referred to as a fictitious business name or F/B/N.

The most basic business structure is a **sole proprietorship**, where one individual owns all the assets and liabilities of the business. For these companies, the owner and the business are the same entity for all practical and legal purposes.

Another type of business entity is a **partnership**, which is a voluntary association of two or more people who mutually agree to operate a business and share the profits and losses. The members of a partnership must pay their share of the company profit on their personal tax returns. General partners have liability for the obligations of the partnership, but there are hybrid partnership/corporation structures that create exceptions to this (e.g., limited liability companies or LLCs). From the standpoint of liability, they are each treated as one entity, with the members liable for their own acts but personally protected from lawsuits directed at the company.

In contrast to a partnership or sole proprietorship, a **corporation** is a business entity acting as a single person distinct from the shareholders who own it. A corporation is essentially considered a legal personhood. The shareholders are compensated in the form of dividends that are declared from company profits. Depending on which country or state the company resides in, the corporation will often have a different name used to signify its legal status. For example, common monikers in the United States include: Incorporated or Inc., Corporation or Corp., Limited or Ltd., and Company or Co. In other countries, the names are very different (e.g., in France corporations are sometimes called SA for *Société Anonyme*, and in Italy they are sometimes referred to as SpA for *Società per Azioni*).

Corporations may be public or private, meaning their shares may be open for sale to the public or not. Generally, companies that are public have reporting requirements that exceed those for private companies, meaning that more information is available for investigators looking into these types of corporations. For example, the quarterly and annual filings for many public corporations are public documents.[55] Regardless of the size and exact structure of a U.S. corporation, general information about the company can be obtained through the applicable state licensing agency.

> *Practical Exercise: Choose an office building you are familiar with and imagine you have been hired by a plaintiff's attorney whose client was badly injured when she slipped and fell on a slippery stair in that building. Assuming the plaintiff's medical fees exceeded $22,000, what is the applicable court where the case would be filed? Who are the names of the possible defendants (consider the owners of the building and property management company, if any)? Where would you physically serve each defendant with the summons and complaint?*

Conclusion

Part V examined basic law, legal procedures and due process, civil and criminal law, legal privacy requirements, and some relevant employment law. As agents of the law, it behooves private investigators to recognize their important role in the legal process and to understand both the theoretical and practical underpinnings of the rule of law and privacy in America. The law is much more than the memorization of key statutes, like the FCRA or the GLBA. It is essential that investigators know and adhere to these important laws, but it is equally important that they understand the broader legal concepts of what constitutes state action and a reasonable expectation of privacy. Similarly, while knowing the trial process or one's state court system is all that an investigator may need to know to traverse that system during a singular investigation—to issue subpoenas, retrieve court records and the like—understanding the model by which all U.S. courts are structured can help guide an investigator in every case, regardless of its jurisdiction.

Lastly, being an agent of the law means being a student of the law, and, since the law is sometimes fluid, this involves being constantly proactive. Upon passage of the Telephone Privacy Act, the federal government did not send postcards to all private investigators who might have been conducting telephone pretexts to alert them that their actions may be illegal; each investigator had to learn the new law on her own initiative. Ignorance is never a valid defense, and the impetus falls upon the investigator to find the line that separates legitimate investigative tactics from those that may land her in prison.

Notes

1. Omnibus Crime Control and Safe Streets Act of 1968, 42 U.S.C. § 3711

2. Electronic Communications Privacy Act (1986), 18 U.S.C. § 2510

3. USA Patriot Act (2001), Public Law 107-56

4. Telephone Records and Privacy Protection Act of 2006, Public Law 109–476

5. Ibid.

6. Federal Trade Commission Act (FTC Act), 15 USC § 45(a)

7. Gramm-Leach-Bliley Act (1999), 15 U.S.C. § 6821

8. Ibid.

9. Fair Credit Reporting Act (1971), 15 U.S.C. § 168, et seq.

10. Fair Debt Collection Practices Act (1978), 15 U.S.C. § 1692

11. Privacy Act of 1974, 5 U.S.C. § 552a

12. Freedom of Information Act (1966), 5 U.S.C. § 552

13. Virginia Freedom of Information Act, Code of Virginia, 37 § 2.2

14. Computer Fraud and Abuse Act 18 U.S. Code § 1030

15. Virginia Code § 18.2-152.4

16. *National Labor Relations Board v. Weingarten* 420 U.S. 251, 1975

17. Civil Rights Act of 1866, 42 U.S. Code 21 §§1981, 1981A

18. Civil Rights Act of 1964, Public Law 88-352, 78 Stat. 241

19. Civil Rights Act of 1991, Public Law 102-166

20. Americans with Disabilities Act of 1990, Public Law *101-336*

21. Rehabilitation Act of 1973, Public Law *93-112*

22. Ibid.

23. Family and Medical Leave Act of 1993, Public Law 103-3

24. Holley, Richard (July 25, 2002). "Legal Guidelines for Contacting Witnesses." Memorandum and speech given at the Metropolitan Washington Employment Lawyers Association on 04/11/08. I was a panelist at this discussion and spoke about the use of private investigators in employment litigation. During a break, Mr. Holley gave me permission to use his material in this book.

25. *Katz v. United States*, 389 U.S. 347, 1967

26. Ibid.

27. State laws also enforce privacy in people's homes. For example, peering into the window of a home would be illegal under Virginia Code §18.2.130, which makes it unlawful to "peep" into a residence or any place where someone may likely be found in a state of undress (e.g., locker rooms, bathrooms, etc.). If the person were actually photographed or videotaped in the nude, then the investigator might also be charged under Virginia Code § 18.2-386.1, which prohibits videotaping naked subjects' without their consent.

28. *Miranda v. Arizona*, 384 U.S. 486, 1966

29. *Daubert v. Merrell Dow Pharmaceuticals,* 509 U.S. 579, 1993

30. Federal Rules of Evidence, Rule 702

31. *Frye v. United States*, 54 App. D.C. 46, 293 F. 1013, 1923

32. "Strengthening Forensic Science in the United States: A Path For-ward" (2008). The National Research Counsel. Washington, D.C.: pp. 3-1 to 3-20.

33. *Weeks v. United States*, 232 U.S. 383, 1914

34. *Mapp v. Ohio*, 367 U.S. 643, 1961

35. *Silverthorne Lumber Co. v. United States*, 251 U.S. 385, 1920

36. *Brady v. Maryland*, 373 U.S. 83, 1963

37. *Giglio v. United States*, 405 U.S. 150, 1972

38. *Jencks v. United States*, 353 U.S. 657, 1957

39. Federal Rules of Criminal Procedure, Rule 26.2

40. Cases with claims between $4,500 and $15,000 may be filed in ei-ther district or circuit court, depending on the type of case. Certain cases (e.g., eviction suits) with claims over $15,000 may also be filed in district court. A full explanation of which type of case must be filed in which specific court is beyond the scope of this textbook.

41. Virginia Courts in Brief. Retrieved from http://www.courts.state.va.us/faq/frame.html on 12/15/08.

42. Ibid.

43. It is further complicated because the Eastern Shore is either referred to as District 2A or District 32, and Virginia Beach is simply referred to as District 2.

44. Handbook for Virginia Grand Juries. Retrieved from http://www.courts.state.va.us/faq/frame.html on 12/15/09.

45. *Hurtado v. California*, 110 U.S. 516, 1884

46. The Answer Book for Jury Service. Retrieved from http://www.courts.state.va.us/faq/frame.html on 12/15/09.

47. The Supreme Court of Virginia and the Court of Appeals of Virginia. Retrieved from http://www.courts.state.va.us/faq/frame.html on 12/15/09.

48. *Pennoyer v. Neff*, 95 U.S. 7141877

49. Business entities are discussed later in the chapter.

50. Code of Virginia, § 8.01-289

51. Rules of Supreme Court of Virginia, Rule 3A: 12 Subpoenas

52. Code of Virginia, § 8.01-296

53. Code of Virginia, § 8.01-299

54. Code of Virginia, § 8.01-293

55. To search for public filings with the Securities and Exchange Commission, the federal agency that regulates securities dealings, visit http://www.sec.gov/search/search.htm.

Conclusion

From conducting relatively straightforward background investigations to more complicated cases involving accidents or fraud, investigators must begin with a solid ethical framework, a thorough knowledge of the law, a methodical system of solving problems, and the acquired technical skill necessary to conduct and document investigations. It is only upon this stalwart framework that an investigator begins applying what most people consider the nuts and bolts of investigating: research, interviewing, and surveillance. Simple knowledge of the methods of observing and experimenting is not sufficient. The private investigative field is fraught with moral pitfalls that require an investigator to exercise self-consciousness with regard to her professional role in society. In addition to these ethical dilemmas, there are also legal pitfalls. Living in a democracy means adhering to the rule of law, respecting privacy rights where they exist, and knowing the legal statutes that apply to investigations.

Conducting investigations in the private sector means solving problems complicated by ethical, budgetary, and other issues. Reliably solving problems always requires a system. By using the scientific method, an investigator with experience conducting investigative research, skillfully interviewing subjects, and performing surveillance will have a roadmap for solving any type of problem in an investigation. But this is still not enough. Performing investigations also requires astute documentation. Reports are often the only tangible work product that clients receive during private investigations. On a fundamental level, private investigation is the business of selling investigative reports to customers. Moreover, investigating is the art and science of gathering evidence, and without the knowledge of how to properly document evidence, its competence may be called into question, thereby negating the fruits of the investigation.

It is an axiom that a private investigator's ethics will be challenged during the course of practicing her profession, and successfully traversing these challenges requires an unyielding moral compass. She must maintain an inner list of moral imperatives—a list that will help her avoid misrepresentation, bias, and conflicts of interest during investigations, and will assist her in upholding her clients' confidentiality. She must also have a sense of the broader role that her profession plays in society. Explicitly defined in each state's licensing laws, what it means to be a "private investigator" encompasses a distinct and important professional identity that has the real potential to impact greater society. To exercise sound moral judgment beyond the cut-and-dry imperative principle, an investigator must be able to weigh ethically the good and bad consequences of her actions both during her investigations and in the sound business practices that she employs in her daily professional life.

Even with a solid ethical framework, however, there are the intricacies of the law to consider. While no investigator is expected to have the knowledge of a lawyer, it is imperative that she understands the principles and theories of the U.S. Constitution and the rule of law, especially the legal safeguards proscribed by the Fourth and Fifth Amendments. It is essential that she understands the structure and workings of both state and federal court systems, the rules regarding service of process, and the myriad types of civil parties and corporate structures. She must also know the procedures for criminal and civil actions, including how they are initiated, tried, and appealed. As a gatherer of evidence, an investigator must understand the rules regarding the admissibility of evidence into court proceedings. Lastly, she must know the major state and federal statutes related to privacy and employment protection.

Successfully solving problems requires the implementation of a system of investigation. It requires first identifying and defining the problem that needs to be solved and then developing and testing a hypothesis using the methods of investigation discussed in this textbook. An investigator may test her hypothesis by conducting investigative research and employing fee-based databases or court records retrieval. She may conduct interviews, carefully interpreting subjects' behavioral symptoms of deception. Lastly, she may conduct surveillance, either covert, overt, or both. By having a disciplined and systematic approach to her investigations, and having an investigative toolbox stocked with all the knowledge and experience required to employ each of the divergent methods of gathering evidence, an investigator should be equipped to solve any problem.

However, even the ability to solve problems is not sufficient; evidence must be properly documented to be actionable in court and to justify the costs associated with conducting private investigations. Constructive testimony begins before the start of an investigation with an investigator's unwavering commitment to good note taking and report writing. An investigator must have thorough knowledge of how to collect and document real evidence, and how and when to take sworn statements and declarations from witnesses. Because private investigation is fundamentally the business of selling investigative reports to customers, if clients are unsatisfied with the quality of an investigator's reports or other documentation, they will seek investigative services elsewhere.

The methods and theories for conducting investigations applies to all investigations, however named or categorized. In this textbook, we discussed the eight different types of investigations named in the Virginia Department of Criminal Justice Services requirements: background, missing persons, criminal, undercover, fraud and financial, insurance, domestic, and accident investigations. The universe of "types" of investigations is practically boundless, but it does not matter. Because with the ethical and legal framework described herein, with a resolute system of solving problems, with the apposite knowledge of conducting research, interviews and surveillance, and with painstaking documentation, an investigator should be prepared to conduct any investigation—ethically, legally, logically, and competently.

About the Author

Philip Becnel is the Managing Partner of Dinolt Becnel & Wells Investigative Group LLC, a private investigative firm based in Washington, D.C. He is the author of the books *Introduction to Conducting Private Investigations* and *Principles of Investigative Documentation*. He has published several articles in investigative, legal, and popular publications including *Time Magazine*, *Westlaw Journal Employment*, and *The Corporate Counselor*. Philip has served as President of the Private Investigators Association of Virginia, and has taught undergraduate courses in criminal procedure, white collar crime, and criminal investigation. He lectures on a wide variety of investigative topics to the legal community and is frequently interviewed by *CNN*, *U.S. News and World Report*, *The Washington Post*, *The Washington Times*, and *The Baltimore Sun* for his expertise and unique perspective. Philip earned his B.A. in Anthropology from George Mason University and his Master's in Criminal Justice from Boston University. He is a licensed private investigator in Virginia, Maryland, West Virginia, and Washington, D.C. Philip lives in Washington D.C. with his wife, Melissa, and their two children, Philip and Ava.

Index

9386241R00147

Printed in Great Britain
by Amazon.co.uk, Ltd.,
Marston Gate.